PROPHETIC DELIVERANCE

The Missing Ministry of Jesus in the Church

TIM MATHER

BCR Press

Dedication

To Katie, my wife and my life.

Table of Contents

Introduction

———◆•◆•◆———

With great fear and trepidation, Dorothy and her friends approach the Wizard of Oz. There are thunderous booms, smoke, and flashes of light. The Wizard's voice roars over the din.

But Toto is not impressed. The little dog scrambles around the curtains, finally taking one in his teeth and pulling it back. And there he is: a mere man moving levers and speaking into a microphone. His next line exposes the sham: "Pay no attention to that man behind the curtain."

If you were Satan, what would be the first element of Christianity you would discredit? I submit it would likely be deliverance, since having even a minimal hold on church people would enable you to disrupt or perhaps just distract them from their true inheritance in Christ.

Like the Wizard of Oz, demons exercise varying levels of control over the Saints personally and corporately, while convincing us they aren't really there.

"My whole family is angry."

"This is the way I grew up."

"We've always done it this way."

"If I just pray more, read the Word more, and go to more services and conferences, I would be acceptable to Father."

"It works for that person but not for me."

"This is just the way it is; just don't tell anyone."

Many denominations and church groups take a firm stance against the very idea that demons might influence or manipulate

Christians. After more than three decades of serving saints who are under the dominion of the Evil One in subtle (and not so subtle) ways, I am convinced, without deliverance, following Jesus is a whole lot of work.

If you are pursuing God to the best of your ability, but your life hasn't worked out the way it seems to work for other folks, then this book is for you. You may even be jealous of your friend's apparent saint-on-roller-skates walk with Jesus. But you don't seem to measure up. Something is wrong with you; something is holding you in its grip. Without deliverance it is next to impossible to shake the Kingdom of Darkness thinking you brought with you into the Kingdom of Light.

You are not alone.

The enemy has convinced many saints he is not real. I have heard folks say their pastor told them there are no demons in America. Others believe demons work only against the heathen and once you say the sinner's prayer, evil influences are no longer in play. Deliverance has been civilized out of what is called the "orthodox" church, thereby providing an open door for demonic influences. As a result, demons run rampant through the pews, stealing, killing, and destroying the Saints at will (John 10:10).

Thus sits the Western Church in the state of fruitlessness and decay we find her in today.

It is time for a house cleaning of epic proportions! It is time to set the captives free—not the captives out there in the world—but the ones sitting in the pews—the religious lost just doing their time in church week after week, still poor, broken, captive, blind, bruised, and believing they are unacceptable to Father.

Read on, weary one! There is an answer in these pages.

Tim Mather

Chapter 1

The Credentials for Deliverance Ministry

———————◆•◆•◆———————

How does one decide to become a proctologist? How is that decision made? Is there a divine call to that profession, or does one just wake up one day and cry, "I must fix fannies!" That's the way I feel about deliverance ministry. It is perhaps the most despised, misunderstood, misused, and most avoided ministry in the whole Kingdom arsenal.

And I am a deliverance minister.

Introduction to Deliverance Ministry

My introduction to deliverance ministry came in my search for help with digestive problems, since for most of my life I had suffered from various intestinal troubles. While serving in the Air Force, I was stationed in Minot, North Dakota, and attended a Christian and Missionary Alliance church there. We were introduced to a traveling evangelist by the name of Bill Putnam, who was part of the congregation, and he offered to pray over me. We set an appointment and I headed for his house.

After a few minutes of small talk, he invited me into his

study and asked me to sit down. He sat directly in front of me and began to pray. Soon, he spoke sharply to what he called demons. I wasn't really thrilled with the prospect of demons affecting me, but I figured he must know what he was doing. He spoke directly to them and commanded them out of me. I remained quiet, seated with my elbows on my knees and my head down. Then, he put his hand on my head and commanded a group of demons to get off my tongue and salivary glands. Immediately, my mouth filled with saliva, but with his hand on my head and my chin pressed to my chest, I couldn't swallow. The saliva continued to fill my mouth while my panic mounted. Was I going to drown in my own saliva right there in his house? Soon, panic overwhelmed my sense of manners and I pushed his hand off my head and sat up. Swallowing never felt so good!

Shortly thereafter, I started to see the fruit of that time of prayer. My digestive problems cleared, and I was functioning normally. I was intrigued.

Over the following months I was privileged to watch my pastor and his leadership team in action. As they attacked demonic strongholds, I was being drawn by the Holy Spirit to get involved. Pastor Dunham allowed me to observe several sessions, and my education in deliverance ministry was in high gear. But what I did not understand at the time was my training in the supernatural had been ongoing from the time I was very young.

Scared Most of the Time

I have always been able to see them. They would appear in one form or another in my bedroom, out of doors, or in any number of places. I was scared most of the time. Somehow I have always been able to see into another realm, the realm of the spirit, to see *demons*.

Some of my earliest memories are of the overwhelming

power of fear filling the room, of peering into shadows and seeing very real faces and figures. My expression of fear brought ridicule from my siblings and denial from my parents that it was real. They were sure I was experiencing the same childish fears most children endure like snakes under the bed or the boogieman in the corner. But when the shadows began to speak to me in audible voices, and when the faces and figures were still there when the light was turned on, I knew these experiences were different. In my fear I prayed the sinner's prayer several times each night to make sure "if I die before I wake, I pray the Lord my soul to take."

Throughout my elementary school years, I spent many nights watching and listening as a panorama of spirits unfolded before me. I was branded a chicken because I was so afraid of the dark. My older brother took great joy in sneaking up and scaring the life out of me. I spent much of the time scared and, as a result, I developed an introverted, introspective side to my personality to make provision for what only I knew was happening around me. I learned to watch intently, to believe my eyes, and most importantly, never to tell anyone what I was seeing. It was when I spent time by myself that I experienced these otherworldly creatures, so I worked hard at not being alone.

Our family moved a couple of times within a short period of time, and as we left the second town, I thought I would escape the frequent hauntings. At our new home, I determined to turn my back on God so He would leave me alone. I was sure He was punishing me for something or other. Of course, by doing this, I inadvertently opened myself up to more of the spirit realm. Between the dreams, visions, and haunts, I thought I was losing my mind.

Jumpy Janitor

In high school, I worked as the janitor for my father's church,

11

where I had hundreds of supernatural experiences. When going into the church to work, I made it a habit to lock all the doors to ensure I was alone so no one could sneak up on me. I often heard voices and footsteps in the silence, so I began playing records on the PA system so loud I could not hear myself scream. I made sure I knew what the last song was on each record so I could sprint to the sound system and put on a new record before there was silence again.

One night, the record stopped before I could reach it and I heard water running somewhere downstairs. I apprehensively approached the downstairs restrooms to find every faucet turned on and water flowing into each sink. I, being the hero, ran from the building, leaving all the lights on and the water running all night long.

From time to time, I would stand motionless as a huge spirit of fear enveloped me. He was so strong I could hardly breathe as he squeezed me like a great python. I could see him as a formless mist approaching me, knowing he had come to torture me. Occasionally, I would break free and stumble breathless from the building. Other times, I would not be able to move until the spirit lifted from me. I experienced wave after wave of nauseating fear as he played havoc with every type of fear imaginable. I shared some of these things with my family and, predictably, they laughed at the stories. So in addition to the regular nonsense of being a teenager, I was plagued by all this supernatural insanity, but I could not tell anyone.

Trying to get to sleep before the manifestations began became my nightly goal. Most of the time it didn't work. Among the myriads of manifestations, one stands out as a turning point in my life because it affected my entire family.

Sometime after midnight while I was lying there trying to get to sleep, a demon appeared in the shape of a hairy frog. He stood watching me for what seemed like eternity. Suddenly, he moved toward me and dove under my covers. I leaped up and ran screaming down the hall and out onto the porch. I woke the whole household. About the time I reached the porch, the entire family burst through the door behind me. I told them, standing in my underwear, it was just a bad dream. They begrudgingly accepted my explanation and shuffled off to bed.

But this time, my covert life got the attention of my parents, and they prayed more diligently for me on a higher level. In fact, unbeknownst to me, my father went to war against the demons that very night. The demons' response was to open and slam doors throughout the house, opening and closing kitchen drawers and cupboards, finally taking the large wooden fork and spoon decor off the wall and putting them against dad's bedroom door. In spite of their antics, my parents persisted and evicted the demons from the parsonage.

Within only a few months, I gave my life to the Lord and was born anew, but the manifestations did not even slow down. In fact, the intensity mounted. As the frequency of the hauntings escalated, something new was opened to me: I began to be aware of the presence of angels. I could see them behind people, on top of buildings, behind the choir on the platform, seemingly everywhere. Over the next ten years I slowly learned how to differentiate between angels and demons and (this may seem profound) *I preferred the angels!*

The Call to Ministry

The year after my conversion, I received my call to the ministry; from that moment, I moved in the opposite direction—away from the call. I ran from the call of God because I was convinced He would have to take me to even higher levels of craziness in the spirit realm. My father would occasionally mention things that happened to him in his ministry, which confirmed my suspicions. I thought I was in the minor leagues of the supernatural and the major leagues—the levels my father was seeing—must be way out there. I didn't want any more of this, so I ran from it.

In the midst of the running, I got married and my new wife began running with me. I ran from job to job, being chased by an unseen pursuer.

Finally, I joined the Air Force and the hauntings became worse than ever. Stationed far away in Minot, North Dakota, God pursued me even there. I was a security policeman assigned to guard missile sites scattered throughout the state. One night my partner and I were checking a missile site, and we both saw something running from the middle of the site. It ran right through our truck, and the engine, lights, and radio all shut down. We stood there like statues for a few minutes until the truck started again all by itself, the lights came back on, and the radio crackled back to life. Startled, we locked the gates and sped away.

There were plenty of hauntings during my duty time, and the same was true off duty. It seemed like one spirit or another would appear in my room nearly every night. The reality of the manifestations grew until my wife began to see them as well. Now we were going crazy together. All the time there were the normal joys, disappointments, confusions, and failings of everyday life mixed into the supernatural, making it a strange life indeed.

Life After Deliverance

This was the point at which I met Evangelist Bill Putnam. Following my deliverance session, I began to see light at the end of the tunnel. When he commanded the unclean spirits away from me and I experienced the manifestations accompanying deliverance, I started to have a sense of hope my life could be brought under some sort of control. That day I not only began my journey into deliverance ministry, but also within a few months,

I surrendered to the call to ministry and began attending classes at a local Bible college.

Deliverance Kindergarten

Something had changed. For reasons which escaped me, I was now able to control the manifestations and hauntings. The spirits were no longer in charge. I began understanding them. I was now able to distinguish between the Holy Spirit and the unclean spirits speaking to me. After all the years of confusion, a light penetrated the darkness and I could see and understand what was happening. From that point on, Father slowly brought my life under control.

During that time, I led a few Airmen to the Lord, and we began a home group to disciple them. This was the beginning of the next level of schooling for deliverance ministry. We grappled with foundational issues of the Word and the Christian life and, at the end of each night we would pray for one another's needs. Almost from the first time there were incredible demonic manifestations within the group. I had no idea how to handle these things, but the Holy Spirit taught me through trial and error. Many times we spent the whole night praying over one another. My friends thought I knew what I was doing; I knew I did not. Demons would speak through them and scare the life out of everyone in the house. Though we did not know what we were doing, occasionally we would see someone set free from bondage.

One night we unearthed an unteachable spirit who manifested both audibly and physically through its host, John. I closed my eyes and saw the unclean spirit had taken the shape of something like an octopus. I implemented the same model Evangelist Putnam used, sitting in a straight chair with the other person sitting with his knees nearly touching mine. I held John's hands as we prayed, and the demon took us for a ride. It took five guys to hold him down while I directed the unclean spirit to come out.

When it quieted down, I bowed my head and began commanding each tentacle out of him, one after another. As I prayed I felt like something was kicking at me but it could only hit my pant leg. I said nothing, thinking it was John. When I finished, Paul had an incredulous look on his face. He recounted what he had seen. He told how he watched as my pant leg flopped back and forth each time I commanded one of the tentacles out of John. He had figured the demon was trying to catch hold of me, so he interceded to keep me safe. The demon was unable to grab me because of Paul's intercession.

That night we learned about the necessity of intercessors. During this formative time, the prophetic nature of this type of ministry began to unfold. From the first, I never asked the demons their names or spoke to them unless there was no other way to get them out. The Holy Spirit taught me to listen to Him, and He told me what I needed to know. This created a dependency on the Holy Spirit, which is still paramount in our ministry today. Operating in the dark, not knowing which way to turn, or what to do when we turned, has kept us in a place necessary to learn the art of prophetic deliverance. That place is utter dependency upon the Holy Spirit alone.

Prophetic Deliverance

My education in deliverance ministry has become a life-long endeavor. Since the early days in 1981, we have continued to learn in every personal deliverance session we have performed. Developing mature, healthy Christians can be a messy endeavor because the work of deliverance ministry is much like building a house. There must first be a digging down into the dirt before there can be any thought of a two story, three-bedroom, Cape Cod. In fact, the Scriptures say without a firm foundation, the entire house is in jeopardy (Matthew 7:24-27).

Deliverance ministry is not showy or admired, rather it takes place "behind the scenes," creating the firm foundation deep in the earth and founded upon a Rock. So, while serving people in deliverance, one is privy to the earthly, dirty, and dark portions of their lives. Such ministry is messy and, many times, beyond filthy in the revelations which are given by the Holy Spirit to release people from the garbage dominating their lives, sometimes even after decades of living a so-called 'Christian life.' These insights into the basest portion of people's lives have produced a series of questions that can be answered only by deliverance ministry.

The Indictment

Our primary question: why is the Western Church in the sad state in which we find her today? I am convinced the scarcity of deliverance ministries has produced generations of anemic, pathetic Christians who are unable to reproduce, unable to live victoriously, and, most frightening, unable to rise above the circumstances of their lives in any significant way to influence the world around them. We are, as a religion, most pitiable. Certainly, there are bright spots in a move of God around the world, but they are the exception rather than the norm. The latest set of statistics of our decline betrays our condition to the world. We are losing pastors by the thousands; we are losing churches by the thousands. We are losing out to cults, psychics, and every sort of mystical, damnable perversion of the true gospel. We are losing, losing, losing.

I Ask You . . .

After all, what is our draw to the unregenerate world? What really makes its citizens want to become part of the Church? Could it be our powerlessness? Could it be the way we drone on through the same worthless liturgies week after week? Or could it be we are no more victorious, no more passionate, no more empowered than the least of those outside the Kingdom of Light? If we are no better than those without, why would they want to come in and live under this system of religious-guilt driving the Church for the past seventeen hundred years? Who needs it?

How is it those in the Kingdom of Light are more easily tripped up than those outside? How is it we of the Light are no more focused and have no better vision than those in the darkness? How is it we are no more healed, no more fulfilled, and no more able to see where we are going than those who are walking in darkness? In fact, those in darkness seem to navigate this terrain in a much better fashion than do we.

For you were once darkness, but now you are light in the Lord. Live as children of light.
Ephesians 5:8

If we are the children of the Light, how is it we are so blind? What is the use of the Good News beyond the obvious hope of someday, way off in the future, moving on to a better place? Is there no hope for *now*?

The Message of Jesus Christ is *the* empowering, capacitating, revitalizing miracle, yet the insanity lies in the percentage of people who claim to be of the Light but are no better off than those in darkness. What is the sense of a message that cannot be proven true today? Where is the logic in choosing the restrictions of religion without taking advantage of the liberties included within? The average Christian is exactly that—average. Where does mediocrity fit in the Message from the Eternal God to mankind? Where does this powerless, debilitating religion of Christianity come from?

The power of God has been exerted upon the earth in the person of Jesus Christ. He must have been born under supernatural

18

circumstances, He must have lived in near obscurity, and He must have died at the hands of his own creation for a greater purpose than is demonstrated by the anemia we call Christianity. Jesus' thoughts on the matter are:

The thief comes only to steal and kill and destroy;
I have come that they may have life,
and have it to the full.
John 10:10

Where is life to the full? Do you experience this life? Do you know anyone within the realms of the Western Church who you can truthfully say is living this verse? With the exception of a few superstars in the Kingdom, where are the common, ordinary people experiencing this life? Is it possible to have it now, or is it reserved for some future time in heaven when everything is perfection? Why does the life of the average Christian more closely resemble the first part of that verse, *"The thief comes only to steal and kill and destroy?"* Our very lives epitomize ones whose goods have been stolen, whose spirit and passion have been killed, and who have been destroyed physically, mentally, emotionally, and spiritually. How can this be? Why is it not as it was in the Biblical accounts? Why is there no protection, no provision, no healing, no life?

By asking these questions am I yearning for the 'health-and-wealth,' 'name-it-claim-it' doctrinal excesses of the past few decades? Certainly not! The expectations of *'life... to the full'* do not demand a perfect existence. The indications are quite the opposite. Jesus said, *"In this world you will have trouble"* (John 16:33). That is His promise to us. Therefore, it is preposterous to believe we are all promised perfect health and perfect wealth, no troubles with our children, or loss of employment. Rather, the answer lies in our *response* to life as it is. This response is the defining element of our lives. James put it well when he wrote,

19

> *Consider it pure joy, my brothers,*
> *whenever you face trials of many kinds.*
> James 1:2

How can this be possible? How is it possible for us to truly count it pure joy, to be thrilled at the prospect of suffering for the Name of Jesus? Have we been so pampered in this culture we cannot see past the immediate into the eternal? Have we walked so long with the silver spoons of privilege and prosperity in our mouths that the slightest bump in the road sends us, along with our godless neighbors, into the waiting rooms of the local psychiatric clinic?

The Good News was intended to have more impact than that. It was given both for life *now* and the future hope of eternity in heaven.

More Questions

Let's take our questions further. Why don't Christians reproduce? Who wants what we have? As a preacher's kid, both of a pastor and a traveling evangelist, I have seen the "best" we have to offer and, if I were in the shoes of those outside the Kingdom, I am convinced I would not so much as glance in our direction. Why? Because defeat and depression are difficult commodities to market to those who are already defeated and depressed.

The message of the Church is "Come and be like us, ain't we happy?" Our services are cookie cutter replicas of the ones we had last week and last year and last decade. Real life is scarce in the average church service, including everything from mainline churches through Charismatic or Pentecostal churches. Some have for a time, but it is soon organized and civilized out in lieu of our orderly, sensible meetings.

Here are more questions. Why are there so many empty seats

20

in churches? Why are there more so-called Christians who opt to skip church than choose to sit through our wonderfully designed religious shows we call "worship services?" Why is church so boring? Why is it so hard to stay awake while the guy up front is performing his liturgical skit? Where is the fun stuff from the Bible? When do we get to see someone raised from the dead? Why is Sister Bertha still sick when God is the God who heals us (Exodus 15:26)? Why do we sing such boring music? Why can't we see the power obvious to everyone in first century Jerusalem?

Why, indeed!

Why the Indictment?

The Church has held the keys to life for twenty centuries, yet we know less power today than we did when the keys to the Kingdom were handed to the first Apostles. We have squandered our inheritance within the taverns of religious pride and bigotry, leaving those outside the Kingdom to die in the chaos in which they were conceived.

How dare we?

The answer is simple: we were not given the whole message. We were called into the Kingdom of Light without the ability to understand the reality of this new dimension. We have created and recreated deceiving and divisive paradigms based more upon human logic than divine revelation in order to secure the differences between us and all those other sects in the Kingdom.

I have always been intrigued by the pride in which certain denominations tout their denominational distinctives. When studying the course requirements for ordination in my ancestral denomination, I was faced with articulating its distinctives. They were theological points that *separated* us from other denominations.

SEPARATED! Astonishing!

Yet by knowing what the distinctives were, then teaching

them, we were fulfilling our denominational mandate to make sure everyone understood we were *not* like the others who called themselves Christians. Instead they were suspect because they did not teach our distinctives. Where are the distinctives between the Kingdom of Darkness and us? Why must the Kingdom of Light be separated and divided like the Kingdom of Darkness?

Am I so idealistic to believe we should all believe the same thing? Yes. It all comes down to one thing: Jesus said if we want to see the Kingdom of God we must be born again (John 3:3). Endless debates about everything else are a waste of breath. We fight about every little point of biblical interpretation out of pride and arrogance, believing we know what is in God's mind, and anyone who disagrees with us is deceived. Yet every other doctrinal issue separating us can be "proven" by its proponents. Take eschatology, or the study of end time biblical events, for example. There are enough positions for everyone in the room without duplicating any of them. One can be firmly pre-trib, mid-trib, post-trib, a-trib, pre-wrath, none of the above, or one of a hundred variations on the theme. Why? So we can proudly say we have figured out God's mind on the matter. Is it important? Does it really matter? Not really. Here's why: Jesus promised He was going to make a place for us, saying:

In my Father's house are many rooms; if it were not so,
I would have told you. I am going there to
prepare a place for you.
John 14:2

We could come with Him some day. The stomach acid generated over this and other issues makes no difference to this truth. We all agree we will live with Him, and *when* it happens is in *His* problem. Everyone who has fought vehemently about these things over the past two thousand years is dead and it has made no difference to them.

22

The Fragmentary Message

So, why does it make a difference to us? Because we are full of pride. We must *know*. If we don't know, we are somehow unsure of our salvation. Remember when you were a baby Christian? Remember when all you knew was Jesus loved you and that was enough? Then recall when some well-meaning brother or sister introduced you to your first doctrine? How it thrilled us to know something others did not. No, it did not begin as full-fledged pride, but as the doctrines piled up, our chests swelled with the hubris of *knowing*. We judge, but never say out loud, "Everyone else in the Kingdom must be stupid because they do not believe what we believe. How can they go on in such a state of deception? How can they be so foolish as not to interpret Scripture the same way our group interprets it? They are probably a cult."

So where is the root of such pride? The root is in an incomplete message. The greatest percentage of the Christian church—from so-called mainline denominations to the aisle running, shouting charismatics—are suffering from the same disease: a fragmentary message.

Let's take it from the top. Our pulpits are filled with well-meaning but insecure people who have personally experienced only a portion of the Good News. They are generally the best of us, yet they are leaving the ministry by the thousands, some falling into sin, others leaving defeated and destroyed by the people for whom they suffered. Within the ranks of the clergy we find many on the edge of nervous breakdowns or other more serious psychiatric conditions, downing mood-altering drugs and trying desperately to survive another day. They carry the spiritual, emotional, mental, and relational loads of their congregations on their shoulders while being incapable of taking care of their own debris.

Their foundation for ministry is training and education.

However, many times those training and educating the clergy are in no better shape. Many of those pouring their wisdom into the next generation of preachers of the Good News are themselves victims of a fragmentary gospel. They dispense water out of broken and polluted cisterns (Jeremiah 2:13), further contaminating the clergy gene pool. The end result of all this is erosion of the Good News, producing anemic, powerless, though well-educated vessels pouring lifeless water onto the dead.

What is the answer? The next few chapters will reveal what, to us and many like us, has been a revolutionary message: the message of wholeness.

Chapter 2

The Foundation for Deliverance Ministry

The Deliverer

Scripture reveals the complete message of Yahweh, God Almighty, the Great I Am to mankind. This truth is revealed in a myriad of ways ranging from direct and specific detail right down to the very name of His Only Son sent to earth to reveal Him. It is not a coincidence the very name of the Son of God means "deliverer." "Yeshua" is the Hebrew name rendered "Jesus" in the Greek text of the New Testament. In the English versions of the Old Testament, "Yeshua" is translated "Joshua." This name also means "deliverer."

It was a day like so many others, a Sabbath soon after Jesus had returned from forty days of war with Satan in the desert. He had gone out into the desert, compelled by the Holy Spirit, to let the Devil know He was about to hurt him very badly. He did so by informing him he no longer had dominion over the earth. This He reclaimed by enduring temptation for forty days at the hands of the master of evil himself.

Having notified Satan, Jesus set about informing mankind of the details of His mission. The understatement of His manner is astonishing. As at His birth, there were no trumpets, no red carpet; just a simple, straightforward statement of His intentions.

Jesus strode into the synagogue and was handed the scroll of the prophet Isaiah. He read the portion we know as chapter sixty-one:

> *The Spirit of the Lord is upon me, because he hath anointed me to preach the gospel to the poor; he hath sent me to heal the brokenhearted, to preach deliverance to the captives, and recovering of sight to the blind, to set at liberty them that are bruised, to preach the acceptable year of the Lord.*
> Luke 4:18-19 KJV

The next line reveals the context: *"Then he rolled up the scroll, gave it back to the attendant and sat down."* He was not given to self-promotion or fanfare. He simply told us, "I'm here to deliver you. Here is my mission statement." It was not only the declaration of the mission statement for His earthly ministry, but also for the entire ministry of His Body, the Church, forever.

In thirty seconds, He changed everything.

There Is Only One Ministry

Churches and ministries across the world develop long strategies and formulas for their ministries. They hire consultants and experts. They spend large sums of money. For what? To determine who they are and what they are supposed to accomplish. Save your money! Jesus just told us the heretofore elusive answer to the all-consuming question.

Deliverance. Not very fancy, is it? It doesn't rhyme; it's not alliterative. He simply said, "I'm here to deliver you."

And we didn't even know we needed deliverance.

Just as the release of the Good News is the fulfillment of the name of the Son of God, His presence, His very being brings deliverance from the snare of the evil one.

> *. . . in the hope that God will grant them repentance leading them to a knowledge of the truth, and that they will come to their senses and escape from the trap of the devil, who has taken them captive to do his will.*
> 2 Timothy 2:25-26

What is the will of the evil one? To trap us into his little kingdom. What is his job?

> *The thief comes only to steal and kill and destroy.*
> John 10:10

We need to be delivered from Satan's mission: stealing, killing, and destroying us. It is so deceptively simple it escapes us. All the programs in the world will not do for us what deliverance ministry will do.

We need deliverance now, and we need it in a few specific areas. First, and most importantly, we need to be delivered from Kingdom of Darkness thinking. The Kingdom of Darkness is the created world and its inhabitants under the Genesis 3 curse. The Kingdom of Darkness is corrupted human nature plus demonic influence. In contrast, the Kingdom of Light (also known as Kingdom of God and Kingdom of Heaven) is purified human nature out from under the curse, set free to emulate our heavenly Father.

Jesus said, *"The Spirit of the Lord is upon me, because he hath anointed me to preach the gospel to the poor."* The first time Jesus preached the Good News He chose an intriguing word to set the precedent for all Good News discussions to follow. He said *repent.* He could have chosen any word and He chose repent, meaning change the way you think. The Good News begins with deliverance from the dominion and power of darkness thinking.

Transitioning from the Kingdom of Darkness to the Kingdom of Light is simply confessing one's complicity with darkness thinking—Scripture calls them sins—and changing one's mind from darkness thinking to light thinking.

What really happens in this process? Our spirits, which were dead in sin, have been brought to life. We were born through water, the water sack within our mother's womb, and now we are born once more, this time spiritually. Our spiritual man is now alive.

How magnificent!

But there is more! We were broken at the very core of our being in the Kingdom of Darkness. So Jesus also said, *"The Spirit of the Lord is upon me, because he hath anointed me to... heal the brokenhearted."* And what about the trap of overwhelming, driving attitudes, habits, and compulsions seeming a little too strong to be just character flaws? Listen to His answer, *"The Spirit of the Lord is upon me, because he hath anointed me... to preach deliverance to the captives."* Could there be more? Even those of us who have received deliverance from the trap of sin can remain trapped in spiritual darkness. We know Father desires intimate relationship with us, yet we are incapable of developing such a relationship. We live without spiritual vision and know the reality of *"where there is no vision, the people perish"* (Proverbs 29:18 KJV). His response is more good news: *"The Spirit of the Lord is upon me, because he hath anointed me... to preach recovery of sight to the blind."*

Many individuals seek the Lord with all their hearts and still find themselves dead inside. They can repent with the best of them, running to the altar time after time and accomplishing nothing. They were so deeply damaged by the Kingdom of Darkness they do not seem to be able to recover. What about them? To them, Jesus says, *"The Spirit of the Lord is upon me, because he hath anointed me... to set at liberty them that are bruised."*

Let's sum up. Jesus declared His intention to all of creation "I'm here to deliver you from all the devastation you have known and to release upon the earth news." If it were told, it would make your hair stand on end. *"The Spirit of the Lord is upon me, because he hath anointed me... to preach the acceptable year of the Lord."*

"Because I came," He continues, "you are now accepted by My Father." This is a reference to the Year of Jubilee, given as a great gift to the Israelites (Leviticus 25:8-17).

What About Getting Saved?

You might be saying, "Yes, but I thought to be part of the Body of Christ we just had to be saved." Nice try. Each word translated "salvation" in the Old Testament comes from the same root word (Strong's Lexicon Hebrew) (3467) yasha` {yaw-shah'} meaning: (bold mine)

1) to save, be saved, be **delivered**
1a1) to be liberated, be saved, be **delivered**
1a2) to be saved (in battle), be victorious
1b1) to save, **deliver**

"Yes, dear brother," you purr, "but we are living in a different dispensation, aren't we?" Let's see if there are any Greek words translated 'salvation' in the New Testament.

Here is the root word translated 'salvation' (Strong's Lexicon Greek) (4991) soteria {so-tay-ree'-ah} meaning: (bold mine)

1) **deliverance**, preservation, safety, salvation
1a) **deliverance** from the molestation of enemies
1b) in an ethical sense, that which concludes to the soul's safety or salvation
1b1) of Messianic salvation

2) salvation as the present possession of all true Christians

3) future salvation, the sum of benefits and blessings which the Christians, redeemed from all earthly ills, will enjoy after the visible return of Christ from heaven in the consummated and eternal kingdom of God.

In both languages, 'salvation' means the same thing: DELIVERANCE. So, why are we so afraid of it?

The Called-Out Ones

The mission statement of Jesus is the foundation for the 'called-out ones' (rendered 'church' in the English New Testament), and it is important we follow His model for ministry. Why name His followers something as awkward as the 'called-out ones?' What could it imply? The first implication is the connection between 'called-out' and 'delivered.' To be 'called out' clearly carries not only a sense of freedom of having been delivered *from* something, but of being delivered *to* something else. These 'called out ones' or, for our discussion, 'delivered ones' are then identified as Jesus' Body upon the earth. This is a brilliant way to show Himself in action upon the earth even though He, Himself, is back in the throne room of His Father in the heavenlies. His 'called out ones' are the portion of Himself remaining on the earth to reproduce His mission statement in others. He perpetuates Himself upon the earth by identifying us with His name: Deliverer, His mission: deliverance, and His family: the delivered ones. Therefore, the mission of the Body of Christ upon the earth is deliverance.

The instructions come from our Head, and the action comes through the rest of the Body. 'Called out' screams DELIVERED! It is the very thing we are, and it is the very thing we do. He is the Deliverer and we are His 'ones' delivered. Our identification tag reads very pointedly, 'Delivered One.' This identification with the Kingdom of Light through the Deliverer makes us members of an exclusive and dangerous club. Remember what the Deliverer came to do?

The reason the Son of God appeared
was to destroy the devil's work.
1 John 3:8b

And how did He make it clear He wasn't kidding? He let the Devil tempt Him for forty days straight. He said, "Give me your best shot!" And He walked away clean. That day the Devil and his work on the earth were destroyed. And more good news: because we are His little brothers and sisters, we are authorized to implement that same defeat by multiplying the number of 'delivered ones.' Each delivery further enforces the victory already won. We are the only vehicles for deliverance upon the earth. So, when we share Jesus in any manner, we share deliverance.

Preaching the Gospel to the Poor

The Spirit of the Lord is upon me, because he hath
anointed me to preach the gospel to the poor...
Luke 4:18a KJV

To put it very simply, the message of the Good News has been targeted toward the poor. Father has made provision for the rich to enter His Kingdom, but the path for them is much more difficult than the one opened before the poor of the earth. Jesus showed us the reality of this when He said:

Again I tell you, it is easier for a camel to go through
the eye of a needle than for a rich man
to enter the kingdom of God.
Matthew 19:24
31

Of course, He follows this statement with one of the absurd realities of the Kingdom:

With man this is impossible,
but with God all things are possible.
Matthew 19: 26

Still, the fullness of the Good News has been given to the poor for very good reasons in the mind of God. Those in poverty know the definition of desperation. Without an understanding of need, there can be no acceptance of the Good News. Unless one has great desperation, the Good News is not attractive. It is out of need and hurt the Holy Spirit draws us to the Cross for deliverance. To those who do not know desperation,

...the message of the cross is foolishness to those who
are perishing, but to us who are being saved it is the
power of God. For it is written: "I will destroy the
wisdom of the wise; the intelligence of the intelligent
I will frustrate." Where is the wise man? Where is the
scholar? Where is the philosopher of this age? Has not
God made foolish the wisdom of the world? For since
in the wisdom of God the world through its wisdom did
not know him, God was pleased through the foolishness
of what was preached to save those who believe.
1 Corinthians 1:18-21

Another reason the Good News targets the poor is a simple matter of logistics. Nearly ninety percent of the earth's population can be classified as financially poor. The rich few rule the many in the lower classes, and spend their wealth upon their own lusts. The rich, by virtue of their economic class, are in greater danger of forfeiting eternal wealth than those over whom they rule. This is the great irony of the message of the Cross. It is the upside-down nature of the Kingdom of God. There are many examples of upside-down thinking in Scripture, such as the place of position and power. If you want to be great in the kingdom of this world, you must accumulate wealth and power. But in the Kingdom of Light the reverse is true:

> *If anyone wants to be first, he must be the very last,*
> *and the servant of all.*
> Mark 9:35

This dichotomy is impossible for members of the dark kingdom to receive.

Only the poor are in the position to look *up* into the Kingdom rather than looking down from some lofty position of wealth and power. Consider the circumstances of Christ Jesus' birth in Bethlehem. How delightfully ironic the Creator of all things, the King above all kings, the Son of the Living God was born into a poor family, born in a cave among the only riches of the poor: cattle. What a delight it is for Father to crush the expectations of the proud by using foolish things to fulfill His designs. If any of us were writing the script for the birth of the King, we would have chosen the most powerful family in the world. We would have chosen the most luxurious surroundings for His birth. We would have announced the news to the kings of the earth instead of those poor shepherds tending their sheep on a hillside.

Ponder for a moment the mind of the One Who created this drama. Contemplate how little we understand His heart. Celebrate the release of the Good News to the poor. Understand our desperate need to receive the Good News. Marvel at His greatness, which cannot ever be impressed by what we are or what we do. Exalt the One Who loves us exactly where we are. And, finally, choose to participate in the delicious irony of the ages: we, who are poor and without resource of our own, are released to receive the riches of the Kingdom of God.

The Spiritually Poor

Preaching the Good News to the poor is not simply a reference to those who are poor financially, but to those who are poor spiritually, relationally, physically, emotionally, and mentally. Those outside of the Kingdom of God are destitute in every sense of the word. They are without hope of eternal life, without hope of peace with God, and without resources for any moral or spiritual life. They are poor where it counts most: they are poor in *spirit*. Their search may lead them from religion to religion, or through any combination of man-made philosophies. This search is the reality of man's poor spirit yearning for God. To be poor in spirit is the inability to satisfy our built-in demand to know God. It is as primal as the need for food or water and it drives man to find God. Many attempt to satisfy their craving by struggling to create their own way to God through some sort of religious activity rather than relying upon the Way provided by the heavenly Father. Each person, poor in spirit, makes some attempt to find God.

Good News, Not Bad News

Most Christian churches and denominations are (or were at one time) quite accomplished at this first portion of the mission statement: preaching the Good News. It has been carried out with great skill and effectiveness over the centuries, resulting in countless revivals, moves of God, and awakenings among the people of the earth. The Church itself survived on the preaching of the Gospel. However, over the centuries, the Message has changed. The word *gospel* means *Good* News. What astounds me is many times the *Good* News sounds more like *bad* news when preached in the form used by many preachers, pastors, and evangelists. Out of their own dysfunction, later generations of preachers have expounded upon the bondage and power of sin without completing the message, revealing it as *good* news. They preach the judgment and the wrath of God against sin, out of their own anger and hurt. They portray a God who is angry and mean. The people they convert by this preaching rarely find life; they simply strive to avoid hell. Consequently, many in the Body of Christ have succumbed to the *harassment* of preaching, rather than being drawn by the Holy Spirit through the Good News. After entering the Kingdom of God, their understanding of the heavenly Father is warped, and relationship with Him is not only futile, but is something to be feared. I believe those who preach in this manner are not preachers of the Gospel. They may say they are and may profess to speak for the Almighty, but their methods bring death where life should flourish.

Jesus came to bring life (John 10:10), not to condemn us further.

For God did not send his Son into the world to condemn
the world, but to save the world through him.
John 3:17

Julio fancied himself to be an evangelist. His intentions were to save the entire human race, yet his methods were atrocious. His version of the Good News was to browbeat people with their filthy lives, repeatedly threatening them with hellfire until they broke under the pressure and prayed the sinner's prayer just to get rid of him. Those who got saved under his 'ministry' were constantly reminded of the guilt and shame of their miserable past and were kept in line by threats of backsliding to that lifestyle. Julio's religious zeal was being used not to satisfy the cravings of the poor in spirit, but as an expression of his own inner pain and anger.

Jesus came to give us life, not to take it from us. Therefore, the Good News must be presented in a manner consistent with His message. The message must not be, "You are going to hell," as much as it must be, "There is hope!"

Most people are sick and tired of themselves. They know there must be more to life than the current fad of materialism or humanism. People are searching for something or someone greater than themselves. Why not show them the way of salvation instead of beating them up with what they already know is wrong?

The news is *good*, and this message of Good News is the foundation for deliverance ministry. It is truly *Good News* to be free from the power of sin in our lives. It is Good News to be free to know the Creator and be part of His family. It is Good News to be privileged to say with the writer,

How great is the love the Father has lavished on us,
that we should be called children of God!
1 John 3:1

The mission statement of Jesus drew an immediate reaction from the religious establishment. This message of wholeness always brings a violent negative response because it touches the very essence of religion. Religion is man's attempt to find God on his own terms. Religion strangles the life out of relationships while failing to touch God. Wholeness, which is the fruit of the application of the complete Good News, breathes life and transforms lives with the powerful truth of healing. Religion develops rules and regulations over time, becoming sacred to their adherents. Once accepted as sacred, the rules become the traditions of men and take on as much or more importance as the true Message. In the end, the Church becomes enslaved to its tradition, liturgy, and ritual, forgetting the simplicity of the Good News.

Any sharer of the Good News must be ever aware of the tendency to over-complicate the Good News. The most effective way to accomplish this is to stay with the core of that message:

For God so loved the world that he gave his one and only Son, that whoever believes in him shall not perish but have eternal life. For God did not send his Son into the world to condemn the world, but to save the world through him.
John 3:16-17

This process begins with leaving the preparation to the One Who is responsible to do it, and keeps our message HIS message. Instead of badgering people into the Kingdom of Light, we must trust the Father to do His part.

No one can come to me unless the Father who sent me draws him, and I will raise him up at the last day.
John 6:43

It does not say we must harass them. He *draws* them. It may sound simplistic, but this is my intent, to keep it simple. Leave what He does to Him, and only do what we are responsible to do: to preach the good news to the poor.

The Full Gospel

Most Pentecostal, Evangelical, and Fundamentalist preachers have done an adequate job of preaching the Gospel to the poor, but few have presented the rest of the message of Jesus: the message of healing for broken hearts; deliverance from the demonic, from strongholds in our minds, from attitudes and habits; restoration of spiritual sight; and freedom from the bondage of a crushed or bruised spirit.

Numerous religious organizations purport to be "full gospel" based upon one distinctive doctrine or another. The reality of the true "full gospel" clearly spelled out in Jesus' mission statement is lost amidst the tangle of doctrinal debate. His message must be returned to the forefront of preaching for the health of the Body. Only the message of Luke 4:18-19 is truly the "full gospel." It cannot be divided up like a turkey on Thanksgiving Day: you cannot choose the drumstick of deliverance and leave the breast meat of salvation for someone else; you cannot push aside the giblets of healing for the broken heart while tasting the thigh of recovery of sight for the blind. This is not a pick-and-choose, one-or-the-other proposal. The mission statement is one complete offer. Yes, it contains six distinct parts, but it is most definitely given as a single inseparable unit. To segment the message is to deprive the saints of the power required to live *now*, to walk in the Light while still living in the darkness of the natural world. Their spirits have been born again, true; they are in possession of eternal life, true; yet their lives are left languishing in brokenness and captivity ruled by Kingdom of Darkness thinking.

Churches are filled with people who have said the sinner's prayer. They do their weekly religious rituals and generally comply with what is being taught. Yet, their daily lives have not been significantly impacted by their religious performance. That is not to say they live in outright disobedience. It means they are continuing to suffer the effects of their past without the relief promised by the Word of God. They have only added God to their lives instead of being released from the dominion of evil and fully given to God. Their spirits are born again, but their minds and hearts are still broken by sin and remain ruled by darkness thinking. The totality of the Good News has been withheld from them. They are struggling to live the Christian life without all the benefits Jesus came to provide. They must be given the whole gospel.

What follows is the *rest* of the Good News story.

Chapter 3

The Rest of the Story

———◆◆◆———

Wholeness

His names will be: Amazing Counselor, Strong God,
Eternal Father, Prince of Wholeness.
His ruling authority will grow, and there'll be no limits
to the wholeness he brings.
Isaiah 9:6-7 The Message

The first part of the Good News is only the beginning of what Father has in store for His children. The rest of the story is found in the remainder of Luke 4:18-19 KJV:

The Spirit of the Lord is upon me, because
he hath anointed me to preach the gospel to the poor;
he hath sent me to heal the brokenhearted,
to preach deliverance to the captives,
and recovering of sight to the blind,
to set at liberty them that are bruised,
to preach the acceptable year of the Lord.

He came to set us free from the bondage of brokenness; He came to free us from demonic captivity; He came to recover our spiritual sight relationship with Father; He came to free us from our bruised and crushed spirit; and He came to declare we are acceptable to the Father. There is so much more to the true Good News than an eventual home in heaven. Jesus provided the means for healing here and now.

We call receiving the entire Good News message the Path to Wholeness. We believe people who receive only a portion or several portions of the message forfeit their privilege to be whole people. Wholeness is what we all need, and the Good News message has it all. Let's take a quick look at the remaining portions of the Good News.

Unhealed Wounds

> *The Spirit of the Lord is upon me, because...*
> *he hath sent me to heal the brokenhearted.*
> Luke 4:18 KJV

Once one is born again, the spirit comes to life. The legal transaction has been completed, and the question of salvation is settled. From that point forward, the born-again person *"work*[s] *out* [his or her own] *salvation with fear and trembling"* (Philippians 2:12) through hearing the teaching of the Word of God and living out that truth. There is a continuing spiritual transformation, which is designed to permeate the whole person, spirit, soul, and body. The effects of salvation should be a radical reconstruction of the entire being. When only the spiritual portion is completed, there is an imbalance in what should be a new creation. This is the reason for so much of the old nature being manifest in churches. When there is disagreement, people's unregenerate emotions are loosed while still under the dominion of the sinful nature. People act out the natural impulses they bring with them from life under the dominion of darkness thinking and attack their brothers and sisters out of fear and/or hurt. When criticism is leveled, the unhealed hurt of the receiver reacts violently to additional injury. Therefore, churches are better known for their fights than they are for the healing they ought to bring.

Often, the greatest unhealed wounds in the Body of Christ can be found in the pulpit. A large percentage of pastors enter the ministry still carrying the wounds from some childhood trauma or other, and they carry those wounds with them throughout their ministries. When a pastor remains wounded, he unconsciously inflicts wounds upon his hearers. Hence, the dysfunction of the church is perpetuated one generation after another. He preaches and teaches out of his hurt. He counsels out of hurt. His reactions to his people flow through the hurt and create unhealthy relationships, either in antagonism or unhealthy attraction. The people who sit under his ministry strain his hurt and wounding message through the grid of their own pain and hear only what their pain will allow. Consequently, the church takes one of two routes: either people attack one another when their own hurts are touched, or they retreat into a kind of religious trance and just perform harmless and ineffectual rituals out of duty.

The latter route provides a false sense of emotional, mental, physical, and spiritual safety for the whole church. Both the clergy and the laity are content to keep the boat on an even keel and quietly "do church." To touch the pain they carry in their emotions or in the depths of their spirits would cause greater anguish, so they hide within the structure of liturgy, which does not permit any connection with our emotional God. They learn to be comfortable within the tradition and structure of religion, whose function it is to appease the sense of guilt we carry without really breaking through to the real issues of our lives.

In contrast to the efforts of religion, the message of Jesus Christ carries more than just a spiritual impact, as powerful and necessary as that may be. The "full gospel" provides real healing for the other areas of our lives connected with, but unchanged by the new state of our spirit. Not only is there relief from sin's devastation in our spiritual lives; there is also power to heal the core devastation as well. Beginning from the starting point of entering the Kingdom of Light, Jesus' message declares broken hearts can be healed. This is the only cure for the destruction at the core of one's being.

Brokenness

*Scorn has broken my heart and has left me helpless;
I looked for sympathy, but there was none, for
comforters, but I found none.*
Psalms 69:20

Life in the Kingdom of Darkness is littered with brokenness. From the time we are born, when the first person we meet slaps our behind and makes us cry, to the cruel loneliness of the old age home, life is full of brokenness. We are broken from relationships; we are broken through all sorts of trauma; we are broken by words and deeds. Everyone carries brokenness. It's time the rest of the Good News is released to those who need it most: church people. We are carrying hurt that not only hinders relationship with other people, but, most devastatingly, hinders relationship with Father.

Out of our hurt, and out of the message of Bad News to which a large percentage of us responded, we hold a perception of Father as a mean man who carries a big stick, prepared and able to strike us at the very thought of misbehavior. We have all heard someone say, "God will get you for that" or "Watch out! God is watching you!" or some such nonsense perpetuating the angry, mean God image. Who wants to have a relationship with someone like that? No one! Out of such trash flows weak, pitiful

Christians who never know the healing they desperately need.

Healing for the Brokenhearted

A man was going down from Jerusalem to Jericho, when he fell into the hands of robbers. They stripped him of his clothes, beat him and went away, leaving him half dead. A priest happened to be going down the same road, and when he saw the man, he passed by on the other side. So too, a Levite, when he came to the place and saw him, passed by on the other side. But a Samaritan, as he traveled, came where the man was; and when he saw him, he took pity on him. He went to him and bandaged his wounds, pouring on oil and wine. Then he put the man on his own donkey, took him to an inn and took care of him.
Luke 10:30-34

The broken man in this parable experiences all religion can offer: an upturned nose, a crossing the street to avoid being sullied by relationship, and a passing by, leaving the broken to fend for himself. But the man could not. That is the nature of brokenness. The cure is found only in relationship. The first relationship is with people who have experienced brokenness and don't even know it. The priest and the Levite demonstrated real damage despite their religious rank when they ignored the man's pain.

The Samaritan man who brought healing to the broken knew the meaning of brokenness. His nationality was despised and demeaned by the Jews. They looked down upon the lowly Samaritans as a second-class race and would not even speak to one of them. He knew emotional hurt; he knew what it was to be broken by others. Out of this understanding, he responded with compassion toward the man on the road.

The help he gave was simple: he came to the man and tended his wounds by pouring in wine and oil. The scriptural picture is clear: wine is a picture of the blood of Jesus, which is for cleansing, and oil is a picture of the Holy Spirit as the healing balm. When we come to the broken, they are very nearly incapable of helping themselves. The most they are capable of is asking for help. The rest is up to us and the Holy Spirit.

Father's Loving Breaking

The sacrifices of God are a broken spirit;
a broken and contrite heart,
O God, you will not despise.
Psalm 51:17

The brokenness received from our natural existence in the Kingdom of Darkness is a counterfeit of the work needing to occur within the confines of the loving hand of Father. The Enemy has taken a wonderful expression of love and turned it into an act of pure hate. Father renders the genuine act of brokenness for our good in the course of being *"conformed to the likeness of his Son"* (Romans 8:29). His process is the privilege of the children of God and is designed to break away the portions of the human nature ingrained in our former life outside of the Kingdom and replace them with a growing likeness of His Son. What an act of love! Scripturally, this is called sanctification. To be sanctified is to be set apart *from* sin, and then set apart *to* Father and His Kingdom.

For us to have any part in the Kingdom of Light, this process must take place. But those who remain broken from their former lives react negatively to the additional breaking, which comes from the Father's hand. If people are not healed of their brokenness when Father immerses them in the pressure of sanctification, He inevitably appears mean, angry, and cruel.

44

Consequently, our warped concept of the loving Father is perpetuated to the next generation, and His true nature is lost in the backwash of pain and anger. When the healing comes, we can allow Father to crush us and to remake us into the person He desires us to be.

Preaching Deliverance to the Captives

The Spirit of the Lord is upon me,
because he hath anointed me...
to preach deliverance to the captives.
Luke 4:18 KJV

The next portion of Jesus' mission statement involves deliverance from those things keeping people in bondage. People are naturally under the influence of the evil one and are subject to his chains. When they come to Christ and are born again, many carry deep bondage into the Kingdom of Light just as they carry in their broken hearts. How does this happen?

Jesus went throughout Galilee, teaching in their
synagogues, preaching the good news of the kingdom,
and healing every disease and sickness among
the people. News about him spread all over Syria,
and people brought to him all who were ill with
various diseases, those suffering severe pain, the
demon-possessed, those having seizures, and the
paralyzed, and he healed them.
Matthew 4:23

In a revival in Argentina in 1954, it was reported that the conversion retention rate (after two years) was over eighty percent. Revivalists in America retain less than ten percent of those who are brought to the place of confessing their sins

45

and coming into the Kingdom. How can this be? What is the difference between the message of those preaching the Good News in South America and the faithful preachers of our country?

In researching these questions, one point stands out: those converted in the revivals of South America were taken through deliverance immediately upon conversion. Generally speaking, the church in America approaches the Good News from a mostly intellectual position. The presentation of the message is rational in nature and appeals to the intellect of the seeker. Little room is given for the reality of the supernatural experience. Therefore, deliverance is assumed. I submit that deliverance *cannot* be assumed any more than a person's brokenness is automatically healed.

There are plenty of good books dealing with the question of demonization and the believer. I will not enter that discussion simply because others have done an adequate job in showing its validity. The Church should be far past that point by now. Still, I think it comes down to something in addition to a theological argument. It comes down to practical experience. There are people who, for all their repenting, for all their weeping and confession, cannot seem to win over certain sins, attitudes, or compulsions. There are certain thought patterns that seem to have power and lives of their own. Though we have walked with the Lord for years, there are walls which cannot be broken through. What are the answers to these perplexing questions? Is it more counseling? Pastoral and even psychological counseling certainly have their place, but the problems remain. What about self-discipline? Aren't these people just too lazy to do what they must do to overcome their issues? The problem with that argument is many of the most demonized people in the church today are overachievers.

The answer comes down to this: deliverance was not automatically accomplished at the moment of salvation. It must be pursued as an experience subsequent to salvation, just as the rest of the Good News must be pursued.

Recovery of Sight to the Blind

The Spirit of the Lord is upon me,
because he hath anointed me to preach...
[the] recovering of sight to the blind.
Luke 4:18 KJV

Those born in the Kingdom of Darkness have no need of sight. Life is dominated by darkness. They are like brute beasts feeling their way around in the darkness. The reality of their lifestyle is never addressed. One can never fully develop when sight is missing. Although sightless people appear to function normally, their lifestyle is completely consumed by the inability to see. As it is with physically sightless people, so it is with those who have been born and have lived in spiritual darkness.

Spiritual blindness is the inability to see into the spirit realm. When Jesus came He broke the power of spiritual darkness and the accompanying blindness. Thereafter, normal spiritual life is replete with seeing, knowing, and perceiving life in the spirit realm. The vehicles for spiritual sight include dreams, visions, prophetic words, words of knowledge, words of wisdom and discerning of spirits through the presence of the Holy Spirit and His work opening our spiritual eyes:

I pray also that the eyes of your heart may be
enlightened in order that you may know the hope to
which he has called you, the riches of his glorious
inheritance in the saints, and his incomparably great
power for us who believe.
Ephesians 1:18-19

This action precipitates an intimate relationship with Father.

It is the purpose of the Father in sending His Son that we be brought back into as intimate and as personal a relationship as He enjoyed with Adam and Eve.

How can we know Him so intimately? Explaining sight to one who has always been blind is a monumental task. Once the blindness is broken, we are more able to *"walk in the light, as he is in the light,"* and the result of that walk is exactly what we have said: relationship— *"we have fellowship with one another, and the blood of Jesus, his Son, purifies us from all sin"* (1 John 1:7). This is the definition of intimate relationship, both with one another and with Father. To walk in the light is to be released from the blindness of the Kingdom of Darkness and to be able to *see* one another and *see* Father in intimate relationship. The light speaks of exposure and transparency. Intimacy is impossible without both.

Jesus reinforced this understanding when He summed up the law and the prophets with this reply:

Love the Lord your God with all your heart and with all your soul and with all your mind. This is the first and greatest commandment. And the second is like it: Love your neighbor as yourself. All the Law and the Prophets hang on these two commandments.
Matthew 22:37-40

These words present the preeminent position of relationship in the Kingdom of Light. In fact, they serve to define Christianity itself. First, the vertical relationship, *"Love the Lord your God with all your heart and with all your soul and with all your mind"* then the horizontal, *"Love your neighbor as yourself."* Both relationships are essential. However, the Church in its quest for intellectual understanding and revelation frequently neglects them. Just as often, one is forfeited for the pursuit of the other.

Both must be pursued and captured for wholeness to come.

The fruit of this intimacy of relationship is the fulfillment of Joel's prophecy concerning the signs of the last days:

> *And afterward, I will pour out my Spirit on all people.*
> *Your sons and daughters will prophesy, your old men*
> *will dream dreams, your young men will see visions.*
> *Even on my servants, both men and women, I will pour*
> *out my Spirit in those days.*
> Joel 2:28-29

The blindness associated with the Kingdom of Darkness having been dispelled, the new saint is given the privilege of "seeing" in the realm of the spirit, the heavenly realms. This sight is given for the *"strengthening, encouragement and comfort"* (1 Corinthians 14:3) of the remainder of the Body, instruction for the present, and motivation and vision for the future. Wholeness in spiritual sight releases saints into dreams, visions, and the prophetic to see, know, and reveal the thoughts and heart of the Father. Those who prophesy and speak for God without coming to wholeness produce rotten fruit.

Healing the Wounded Spirit

> *The Spirit of the Lord is upon me, because he hath*
> *anointed me… to set at liberty them that are bruised.*
> Luke 4:18 KJV

The concept of wounds in one's spirit may be foreign to some. Depending upon the translation you prefer, several words are used to communicate this destruction. The NIV uses "crushed" and the KJV uses "broken" and "wounded" to express the same idea: destruction in the spirit of the person.

A man's spirit sustains him in sickness,
but a crushed spirit who can bear?
Proverbs 18:14

A cheerful heart is good medicine,
but a crushed spirit dries up the bones.
Proverbs 17:22

You may know crushed people, or you may be crushed yourself. Crushed or wounded people are more than just hurt emotionally. They are deeply broken. The pain is not just emotional. It is down in the deepest portion of the belly, and it nearly takes the breath away. A crushed person may have resigned himself or herself to the brokenness. Most develop coping mechanisms to hide their pain from others, as well as to just make it through another day.

From where does such deep destruction come? It can always be tracked back to some life-altering destruction such as childhood sexual, verbal, or physical abuse, some horrendous betrayal, or some other prodigious act of devastation. Either it has been imposed upon the person or the person acts it out. The Good News, however, contains hope for this truly lost soul. Jesus' mission is *"to set* [him] *at liberty."* This is true deliverance. The wounds weigh so heavily upon the spirit of the person, life is consumed by the weight. The Good News is this weight has been borne by another, so *liberty* can be the standard of life in the Kingdom of Light.

Father is not just concerned about the wounded; He has focused His very attention upon them. This is how it is:

The Lord is close to the brokenhearted
and saves those who are crushed in spirit.
Psalms 34:18

Father *"is close"* to the broken. Not only is there healing; there is intimate relationship just waiting for that person. This, too, fulfills the relational aspect of the Good News. The Creator of all things, the Great I Am, the Ancient of Days, Almighty God desires to be close to us.

Amazing!

Summing Up the Good News

> *The Spirit of the Lord is upon me,*
> *because he hath anointed me...*
> *to preach the acceptable year of the Lord.*
> Luke 4:19 KJV

The final section of the mission statement of Jesus Christ presents a word picture to sum up everything given through His ministry and the continuing ministry of His Body, the Church. The *"acceptable year"* is a direct reference to the Year of Jubilee explained in Leviticus 25. It was to be the Sabbath year of Sabbath years, the fiftieth year. In the Year of Jubilee, all the bought or sold land would revert to the rightful, hereditary owners. Debts were cleared, and slaves were set free. It was a year of total acceptance, of joy, of jubilee. Jesus' mission statement included the promise of Jubilee for those who accept His message of Good News. The promise is liberty from every sort of bondage, from the debt of sin, from emotional destruction, from spiritual bondage, from spiritual blindness, and from deep woundedness. It is the promise of acceptance by the Father: He truly receives us as His children. We, by accepting His Son, receive sonship ourselves and shed the scourge of sin under the dominion of darkness. The acceptable year of the Lord is the limitless abundance of grace Father has extended to those who receive His Son.

The Centerpiece of the Message

It is important to recognize deliverance as the centerpiece of the entire message of salvation. We begin, on one hand, with *"good news to the poor"* and *"healing for the brokenhearted,"* and end with *"recovery of sight to the blind"* and *"liberty for the deeply bruised."* Right in the middle we find the one thing all these parts revolve around: *"deliverance to the captives."* It could not be clearer, although first things are first (that is, the receiving of the Good News), deliverance takes on the preeminent place in the complete message of salvation. Therefore, without following through with the ministry of deliverance, one cannot be truly whole.

Chapter 4

Liberation from the God of the Tangible

———◆•◆———

Supernatural Paradox

Deliverance ministry is a strange thing. Deliverance, more than any other ministry of the Body of Christ upon the earth, forces believers to embrace the unknown, supernatural realm. The Western church has so organized and secularized its way of thinking about the supernatural that deliverance flies in the face of what we now know to be true intellectually. We have become unbelievers. We have become entrenched in Kingdom of Darkness thinking, bowing to the influences of corrupted human nature and losing touch with the supernatural. Deliverance ministry is a casualty of that loss because we must connect with the reality of a realm beyond our senses, beyond sight and sound, beyond intellectual comprehension, and out of the control of our temporal-based world-view. The Church, fearful to appear out of touch with the times, has lost touch with the very thing setting it apart from any other organization or religion on the face of the planet: the supernatural.

On one hand, all Christians inherently believe in the reality of the supernatural since we claim the born-again experience. We are convinced at one level or another that Jesus Christ is Who He says He is, and the Scriptures are true. Without apprehending Him with our senses, we believe there is a God and He is concerned about us. We claim to speak to Him in prayer. Some of us weep over the death of His Son, while others leap, fall over, laugh, dance, or sing when they join with other Christians. We recite stories from the Bible about angels and demons, some even manifesting in human form, without batting an eye. Our whole religious experience is based upon a history of supernatural encounters, from the creation recorded in the first book of the Bible to the account of the apocalypse in the chapters of the last book.

Yet many of these same Christians have difficulty acknowledging the presence, or even the existence, of supernatural entities today. Their minds refuse to believe, outside of Biblical times, anything remotely resembling a spiritual realm exists. Somehow it seems acceptable for an angel to visit the Virgin Mary, Abraham, or other Biblical character, but it is another thing entirely when told of the same kind of experience occurring in a modern, "civilized" society. The activity of both the evil and the righteous spiritual realm in everyday life is dismissed or denied entirely. Angels, after all, are for Bible stories told in Sunday School. It is inconceivable one might encounter the same angelic being in a three-bedroom ranch equipped with running water, electricity, and sporting a two-car garage all situated conveniently on an acre and a half in the suburbs.

Yes, we Christians are an odd lot.

This book is written especially for these peculiar people who have a selective belief system all wrapped up in a little safe, comfortable, intellectual, religious package. Sure, you believe the things required to be a good church person, but let's not become some sort of fanatic! Through years of deliverance ministry, we have found it is prudent to walk gently around you semi-supernatural believers. Most of you simply have not been taught the reality of the spiritual realm as part of the weekly regimen of your church. Others of you are fearful of getting "out of balance" and moving off on some tangent from the true Word of God, as if acceptance of the supernatural in your daily lives would cause you to stray from "sound doctrine." Still others put stock only in what you can see and have no time for all that supernatural mumbo-jumbo. It is for you I write, to ask you not to prejudge the issue anymore, but to seriously and joyfully consider these few pages in light of what *might* be true. If you will risk your belief system for a little while and read this whole book, you may just come away with a balanced, scriptural approach to the spiritual realm in general, and deliverance ministry in particular.

Spirit Is More Real Than Flesh

Our first stop on the journey into the Unknown is Philosophy 101. The statement reads: "Spirit is more real than flesh." Consider this statement for a moment. In our technological, scientific world a statement like this may cause confusion. It shouldn't. It is not just a worthless philosophical discussion. Rather, it is the essential revelation for any discussion of deliverance ministry.

Follow the logic. Ponder Genesis 1:1, *"In the beginning God created the heavens and the earth."* Then ponder John 4:24, *"God is spirit, and his worshipers must worship in spirit and in truth."* Now, if God is spirit and He created the heavens and the earth, and the rest of Genesis one and all of chapter two show He created not only the earth itself, but everything upon the earth, then which is more real? Spirit is more real. God, as Spirit, existed in eternity past, long before He created anything physical or tangible. Spirit is the source of all things. Spirit is more real than flesh. Why, then, do we place so much emphasis upon the tangible? As humanity has progressed, we have created machines, explored not only our own planet, but deep into space. We have built upon the recorded knowledge and wisdom of the humans before us until that cumulative understanding has become our god. Let's call him the "god of the tangible." The true worship of this god requires a strict adherence to the tangible, to reproducible results, to what we may understand through the scientific method. The god of the tangible demands reality can always be measured and studied by its priests. Within the safety of its doctrines we have no need of anything that cannot be grasped by our senses. The result of worshiping the god of the tangible is a stubborn refusal to accept what cannot be touched, smelled, seen, tasted, heard, or reproduced in a laboratory setting under controlled conditions.

Spirit cannot be apprehended by the senses or controlled by human intelligence or logic.

Therein lies the difficulty. We Christians, who should embrace the supernatural realm, are the greatest hindrance to releasing the liberating force of supernatural deliverance ministry upon the world by our stubborn refusal to give up our former god, the god of the tangible. We bring our understanding of the god of the tangible into the Kingdom of Light and demand the principles of this new Kingdom adhere to the laws of our former god. We trust only our senses to grasp the laws of the new Kingdom. We rely upon our old perceptions as a foundation from which we build our understanding of the Kingdom of Light. And we have the gall to indict Father because He does nothing for our circumstances. That is what the writer meant when he said,

Trust in the Lord with all your heart and lean not on
your own understanding.
Proverbs 3:5

Our own understanding resists the precepts of the Kingdom of Light and, unless entirely altered, it not only has the power to keep us in the grasp of the god of the tangible, but thwarts the process of salvation in our lives. This condition is appalling when it damages the operation of the Spirit in individuals. When individuals under the influence of the god of the tangible are placed into leadership in the Kingdom of Light, they keep the entire Church in bondage. As the local church cannot escape, so the universal Church is held in check.

But our God is not the god of the tangible! Our God is *"the God who gives life to the dead and calls things that are not as though they were"* (Romans 4:17). He is the God of the infinite; He is the God of the unseen, the unknown, the unfathomable. The laws of physics or the laws of mathematics do not hinder Him. He is the Creator of them. He is not in bondage to the limited understanding of men. He clearly sees those things are mysteries to men and makes them known to us: *"There is a God in heaven who reveals mysteries"* (Daniel 2:28).

It is this God who brings us deliverance from what enslaves us.

The Credibility Crisis

Deliverance ministry, with the possible exception of the practice of speaking in tongues, is the most controversial ministry of the church. Because the god of the tangible has been given jurisdiction over our doctrinal and liturgical structures, deliverance is looked upon with scorn by intellectuals and with fear by the uninformed. In either case, it has become a practice to be avoided. Even those who move in the other Gifts of the Spirit (1 Corinthians 12) use deliverance only in very limited ways. Anything more powerful is treated with contempt. They lump all deliverance ministries together with some of the outrageous attempts made famous by the media and poke fun at the whole ministry.

Admittedly, throughout church history there are accounts of the misuse and outright abuse of the authority used for casting out demons. Two of my own ancestors, Cotton and Increase

57

Mather, were involved in the Salem witch trials and wrote extensively on the subject of witchcraft and the supernatural. In their time, just as in ours, people were embarrassed, hurt, devastated, and even murdered in the name of deliverance from evil spirits, all because of the abuse of spiritual authority. Many church leaders have misused the spirit realm to accomplish their own ends. It has been used as a control mechanism to instill fear and solidify the clergy's hold on the lives, and, more specifically, the purse strings of the people. These practices have been well documented from the early years of the Christian Church, even throughout this century. We look back and shake our heads at their silly superstitions and feel confident we are so civilized these things could not happen today.

I once spoke on deliverance before a group of so-called 'Spirit-filled' pastors and evangelists. I was given five days, one hour a day, to share our deliverance ministry and offer its life-giving fruit to the ministries represented. To my utter amazement, I had to spend most of my time trying to convince my hearers deliverance ministry was a real and needful addition to the tools they already used for ministry. I defended my position from one attack after another, and I heard argument after argument full of fear and ignorance concerning the workings of the spirit realm. I came away feeling deflated. How could people be set free from the entities harassing them if the very ones commissioned to set them free held to their theological stances rather than waking up to the reality of the problems their people were facing?

After several hours of standoff, I finally shared from my heart the reality of deliverance in our own lives. Although the evangelists among them held firm in their denial, I could see several of the pastors knew what I was talking about. Nearly all of them had been frustrated and stymied in counseling situations with people in their churches, having no answers either in the psychological realm or biblical realm. They were at a loss to understand what was happening to hurting people and needed the tools to unlock the prisons in which they were bound. This need transcends theological training and argument. It resides in the realm of the spirit.

Even in recent history, the Charismatic movement came under tremendous fire for the widespread use of deliverance ministry. Many of the participants during those years were operating in uncharted waters and doing the best they could. Because of the nature of the supernatural and the inability to adequately understand what is happening in that other realm, they reverted to bizarre methods right out of the Dark Ages to achieve deliverance. Some taught the use of vomiting up demons (Yes, real vomit! In fact, plastic bags and/or garbage cans were sometimes provided at the front of sanctuaries for vomiting during deliverance).

Others taught that demons came out when the person yawned or burped. Still others felt deliverance should resemble the totally ridiculous antics in the movie *The Exorcist*. These well-meaning people were reacting to spiritual manifestations with methods based entirely on Kingdom of Darkness thinking. Whether any real deliverance took place in these sessions is a question for Father.

As a consequence of these abuses, deliverance ministry is once again suffering a credibility crisis. Most Christians have one horror story or another to tell about a person or group that was fine until they started messing around with deliverance. The tale usually goes on about how someone went completely off the deep end into heresy and today the group is either disbanded or he is off in some doctrinal black hole. However, deliverance, done properly, is no more threatening than serving communion or leading someone to salvation. In fact, it is normal Christianity.

If I drive out demons by the finger of God, then the kingdom of God has come to you.
Luke 11:20

Deliverance Without the God of the Tangible

We have come to despise the god of the tangible and its darkness thinking, especially in our deliverance ministry. When we started doing deliverance, there were manifestations and outrageous behavior by both the participants and the demons. Over time, we found manifestations were not necessary for making sure the demon had been cast out. In fact, we found deliverance is best experienced without any tangible manifestations at all.

Whenever deliverance ministry without tangible evidence is mentioned, objections are inevitable. The basic problem is that immediate proof of deliverance is not necessarily evident. One may be required to wait weeks or even months to see the fruit of a deliverance session. Skeptics and unbelievers demand immediate empirical evidence or they are not convinced.

This is confirmed by the so-called exorcisms shown on television. In our obsession with high drama, we are not convinced unless the demon screams through the person. There is always a lot of commanding and dramatic action by the exorcist, as well. He is usually seen pressing a crucifix into the forehead or chest of the client until he leaves red welts. He sprinkles water on the person and shouts commands. All this is playing to the audience! What Biblical precedent do we find for any of those things? None. We are simply reacting to a scary process with tangible tools.

When that type of exorcism is done, at what point do those involved know it is time to stop? They stop when the client is so exhausted he or she falls asleep or the demon simply ceases to manifest. They depend upon the tangible evidence rather than upon what is true in the spirit realm. Where the Spirit of God is not depended upon for revealing the truth, the truth must be determined by external, physical evidence.

From time to time you may come across a case of severe demonization and be able to see or hear irrefutable manifestations, but in deliverance ministry, evidence is scarce. The reason? If done properly, deliverance is an extremely serene ministry whose fruit is transformed lives rather than spinning heads or eerie voices. Reliance upon manifestations to prove demons are resident elevates the stature of the demon and degrades the person suffering under its dominion. Deliverance ministry has turned into something akin to a sideshow attraction at the circus. Most abusers of deliverance ministry rely upon the demons to demonstrate their existence rather than operating through the Gifts of the Holy Spirit given for just such ministry. They then cast them out based upon the tangible proof of manifestations. If you rely upon the demonic for proof, you will be open to deception. In their fainthearted misunderstanding, many deliverance ministers have missed the true joy and power of watching the fruit grow in the weeks, months, and years following the session.

A Supernatural Approach to Deliverance Ministry

Farmers are the most optimistic people in the world. They never believe what they see. They believe next year will be the year the crop will come in abundantly, the rain will come soon, and it is all about to get better. Every spring they enthusiastically spend most of their hard-earned capital to buy seed and bury it in the dirt. For the next few months, they wait to see the first sprouts from the ground, and then grow into healthy, mature plants. They are never convinced the pests or weeds will win. They may not see it with their eyes, but they know in their hearts the crop will grow in spite of what is seen or not seen on the surface.

Doing Prophetic Deliverance ministry is much like being a farmer. You do not have to see it with your human eyes or grasp it with another of the senses to know it is happening. In fact, you must NOT rely upon what is seen. You must rely upon something beyond your control or understanding to ensure the growth of the fruit. Those we train for this type of ministry surprise us. Most are more willing to believe what is being said or done by a demon than what has been said or done by the Creator of all things. Our confidence must be in Him and in His promise to set the captives free, whether we see it with our natural eyes or not. Deliverance must be a supernatural ministry based upon supernatural principles, using supernatural methods, relying upon our supernatural Father to supernaturally perform what He has promised. If we leave it to the god of the tangible for verification, we circumvent the true supernatural act of deliverance.

When someone is born from above, there is no empirical evidence salvation has taken place. Some may expect the person should weep when confessing sin. Does that mean no regeneration has occurred if there are no tears? I do not think many would stand by that argument. Because deliverance is a continuing work of regeneration, it stands to reason no outward evidence should be expected. Just as we do not see the sin leave when it is confessed and rejected, so we do not expect to see the demons exit when they are cast out. When Jesus dealt with demons, He did not spend time convincing the spectators of the reality of the demonic; He simply cast them out. He was not concerned whether they believed what He was doing was real because the worldview of the people at that time included an understanding of the supernatural realm. Since then, that understanding has been lost in the quest for the god of the tangible.

Supernatural, Not Superstition

Some years back, I heard a noted international evangelist mocking deliverance ministry in all its excesses and blunders. He said it was all superstition and believers should come out of the Dark Ages. He chose several areas of what is commonly called "spiritual warfare" and demeaned both the concepts and the people who teach them. He declared it was not even in the Bible. He was adamant none of these things were needed, salvation took care of it all, and it was a lack of faith to believe otherwise. The crowd heartily received his point and they clapped and cheered his daring "exposé" of deliverance ministry. Yet, sometime later, while praying with an individual in a prayer line, this evangelist was heard to shout, "Demon, come out!"

He made my point exactly. Deliverance may not seem civilized or current, but it is nevertheless necessary for effective ministry. Although it may appear to be something weird or full of superstition, it is *essential* to the life of the believer that those who are bound by demonic forces undergo deliverance and be set free. Even those who hold theological stands against it find they are ultimately at the mercy of the spirit realm. Then, with few hard-fast rules to follow, they do the best they can to assist seekers in their quest for freedom.

We are not advocating some sort of demon-hunter society valuing the hunt over the person. Rather, we are encouraging a ministry that can rebut superstition and legend. It is a shrewd policy of the Enemy to make a portion of the very work of salvation, which sets people free from his power, appear to originate from *him*, and therefore be shunned by the very people who need it the most. The Enemy's best weapons against us are fear and ignorance.

We are fearful of many things, not the least of which is the fear of being a fanatic. Fanatics are viewed to be out of balance and out of touch with the "sound doctrine." The first word to escape the skeptic's lips is "cult." This word is used to define organizations and theologies defying what has been designated as acceptable thought for a particular group. In this manner, the Enemy is effective in redirecting the real issue from understanding to one of fear. This fear cultivates an impenetrable wall of ignorance in that people will never be open to something which they have been taught is cultic, weird, or out of the mainstream of orthodox thinking.

Theological thought itself is mostly a collection of ideas encased in the fear that there could be something about the supernatural realm we cannot comprehend, canonize, or categorize. All religious organizations are the same. They set up a system of thought and defy anyone to challenge it. If one should dare to embrace a scriptural principle not previously categorized, canonized, or comprehended by a predecessor, then it is rejected out of hand and ignored. That way, the theological system may stand as a rock, impenetrable and firm against the onslaught of what may turn out in the end to be simple biblical truth.

How do you think denominations can remain at such odds with one another? The reason is their rigid, unyielding fear of theological understanding. Once it is written down as a belief system, it becomes the law. Interesting thought, isn't it? The law. Is it not true the Spirit is now the determining factor for truth rather than the written law of men? Consider Galatians 5:18, *"But if you are led by the Spirit, you are not under law."* Does that mean any written theology is evil? Not at all. But it does mean the Spirit of God makes the determination regarding that written code and He is always depicted as something which, though real, is impossible to tangibly hold. He is characterized as wind (John 3; Acts 2), water (Isaiah 44:3), and oil (Matthew 25). He is as inexplicable as all those things and more. So why do we insist we know all there is to know about Him? We are afraid *not* to know.

The Only Ministry

Deliverance ministry is about the captive. It is not about controversial methods or doctrinal issues. Jesus' earthly ministry was a reflection of this philosophy. He came out of the norm of religious society with a message of deliverance, not just from evil spirits, but deliverance from *anything* that enslaves. He came for one reason: we need deliverance. We are in need of salvation (deliverance) from the trap of sin. We are in need of salvation (deliverance) from the bondage of emotional destruction. We are in need of salvation (deliverance) from the bondage of the demonic. We are in need of salvation (deliverance) from the bondage of spiritual blindness. And we are in need of salvation (deliverance) from the bondage of crushed, bruised spirits. We need *"the hope that God will grant* [us] *repentance leading* [us] *to a knowledge of the truth, and that* [we] *will come to* [our] *senses and escape from the trap of the devil, who has taken* [us] *captive to do his will"* (2 Timothy 2:25-26).

In actuality there is only one ministry: deliverance. Our Deliverer has come to destroy the devastation the evil one has wreaked upon the human race. *"The reason the Son of God appeared was to destroy the devil's work"* (1 John 3:8b). What is that work? *"The thief comes only to steal and kill and destroy"* (John 10:10) and *"Your enemy the devil prowls around like a roaring lion looking for someone to devour"* (1 Peter 5:8). The mission statement Jesus declared in the synagogue that day (Luke 4:18-19) declares His intention loud and clear: He came to deliver us from the chains and the prison that enslaves and binds us. He came to set us free.

So if the Son sets you free, you will be free indeed.
John 8:36

Chapter 5

Definition of Basic Terms

———————◆•◆———————

Before entering any discussion of deliverance ministry, it is important to define the terms used to describe certain entities, events, and other elements involved in deliverance ministry. I am always amazed at the lack of understanding among believers regarding even the most basic of terms. Below you will find most of the specific terms and definitions under which we will operate.

Deliverance

For the sake of this study, we will define deliverance in the narrowest of terms. Deliverance is the action of a believer upon another person to cast out or command away one or more demonic beings. Jesus' earthly ministry can be defined by three main deeds. First, He preached the Good News. Second, he healed the sick. And third, He cast out demons. His mission statement found in Luke 4:18-19 presents deliverance as one of six major tenets of the faith. In Jesus' own words, He declares the very first sign marking believers from that time forward, was the ministry of deliverance:

*And these signs will accompany those who believe: In my name **they will drive out demons**; they will speak in new tongues; they will pick up snakes with their hands; and when they drink deadly poison, it will not hurt them at all; they will place their hands on sick people, and they will get well.*

Mark 16:17-18 (bold mine)

Satan

This is from the Greek word *satanas*, meaning "adversary," and "one who resists." He is the fallen archangel Lucifer who, in eternity past, decided he would *"...make* [him]*self like the Most High"* (Isaiah 14:14). Everything Satan does is aimed toward that end. He has become the master counterfeiter, counterfeiting the Most High in each action, in each statement, in each purpose. He counterfeits Father's omnipresence by use of his band of demons. It appears as if he is everywhere just as Father is. In fact, most of Christendom believes he is omnipresent. In our travels, I have witnessed many people who speak to him in their prayers. Possibly you have uttered the seemingly powerful words, "I rebuke you, Satan!" The fact of the matter is Satan can be in only one place at a time and it is most likely *not* next to you. If Satan himself has visited you, then you must be a most powerful warrior. Satan's duties keep him pretty well occupied in the heavenlies before the throne of the Father: accusing us and running around on the earth. Look at Revelation 12:10-12 (bold mine):

*Then I heard a loud voice in heaven say: "Now have come the salvation and the power and the kingdom of our God, and the authority of his Christ. For the accuser of our brothers, **who accuses them before our God day and night,** has been hurled down. They overcame him by the blood of the Lamb and by the word* *of their testimony; they did not love their lives so much as to shrink from death. Therefore rejoice, you heavens and you who dwell in them! But woe to the earth and the sea, because the devil has gone down to you! He is filled with fury, because he knows that his time is short."*

Stop wasting your breath yelling at someone who is not there. The fundamental purpose of Prophetic Deliverance is, by the Spirit of the Living God, to identify and speak to the particular spirit harassing the individual. Stop rebuking the demonic beings not even in the room. Speak to the Father *about* them. If the demonized person is not within earshot, the demons will not be able to hear. If they can be omnipresent, then they and their master, Satan, truly have succeeded in becoming *"like the Most High."* If the unclean spirit to whom you are speaking is not present, then he cannot hear what you are saying.

Satan's purpose toward mankind is *"to steal, kill, and destroy"* (John 10:10). His motive is counterfeiting what Father is and is doing. In counterfeiting the Father, he is only able to bring destruction. He can never solve the problem or make the situation better, unless he does so to further enslave the recipient. His heart is set on destroying those whom the Father loves. The entire population of the Kingdom of Darkness is arrayed in this manner. Therefore, it becomes a serious matter when one opens the door, making room for those forces to gain a place in one's life.

Devil

This word is from the Greek word *diabolos* meaning an "accuser," and "a slanderer." This is an indication of Satan's employment as *"the accuser of our brothers"* (Revelation 12:10b). It has been used incorrectly in a general sense referring

68

to demons, but there is only one "devil" and his name is Satan.

Demon

This is from the Greek word *daimon* meaning an "evil spirit being inferior to God and superior to man." Demons are evil angels, part of the contingent cast from the third heaven with Satan during his rebellion against the Father. They are not, as some teach, disembodied spirits walking the earth in search of a place of rest. There is no Biblical evidence for this idea. They are simply evil angelic beings, and, like their leader, they are not creative beings. They do not create anything; they simply manipulate people and events to make it appear as though they do. Their primary duties are to harass and frustrate the Children of God.

At times, they are unwillingly used by Father to accomplish His own ends. We find this in the story of King Saul when an evil spirit was sent to harass him:

Now the Spirit of the Lord had departed from Saul, and
an evil spirit from the Lord tormented him.
1 Samuel 16:14

Father uses them both against His own people to discipline them, and against the wicked to destroy them:

He cast upon them the fierceness of his anger,
wrath, and indignation, and trouble,
*by sending **evil angels** among them.*
Psalm 78:49 KJV (bold mine)

As a group they are referred to as the *"spiritual forces of evil"* (Ephesians 6:12). Deliverance ministry, for the most part, takes place against this lowest level of demonic spirit.

Heavenly Realms (Heavenlies or Places)

The scriptural definition of "heaven," the "heavenlies" or "heavenly realms" is made clear through three different types of "heaven." They are the expanding reality of the universe. In the temporal or physical realm, we find plenty of references to what we will call the "first heaven." For example, Psalm 19:1 makes reference to the physical sky, or the firmament when the Psalmist writes, *"The heavens declare the glory of God; the skies proclaim the work of his hands."* This is undeniably the blue sky above. The first heaven is the temporal or physical reality. In terms of function, it is the most finite. Under this heaven, we are confined mainly to the physical reality, whereas in the other two, the spiritual reality is primary. In the first heaven, then, the spiritual aspects of reality are limited to this reality alone. There is seldom a crossover into one or the other of the heavenly realms.

Scripture then takes us into what is called the "third heaven." Paul mentions it in his writing to the Corinthians: *"I know a man in Christ who fourteen years ago was caught up to the third heaven. Whether it was in the body or out of the body I do not know—God knows."* (2 Corinthians 12:2) We find it mentioned again when Jesus was teaching the disciples how to pray: *"After this manner therefore pray ye: Our Father **which art in heaven**, Hallowed be thy name"* (Matthew 6:9 KJV [bold mine]). This appears to be the dwelling place of the Father. It is paradise, the presence of the Almighty. This is the ultimate, infinite reality— the whole thing, all reality, God's reality. It is His realm, the realm where His throne is located, opened for us to occupy for all eternity.

There is another heaven, a "second heaven" (though not mentioned in Scripture it must be there for there is a THIRD heaven) that is nevertheless real and functioning.

Whereas the first heaven is the physical reality, the second

70

heaven is the spiritual reality or the reality of the spirit realm affecting the earth. It does not extend into the realm of the third heaven, but is limited to the area surrounding the earth itself. It is the reality where angels and demons function that is less finite than the first heaven and more finite than the third. It is a realm between the one occupied by the Father and the temporal one occupied by all physical life. It is the realm in which all spirits dwell. It may be generally understood as a fourth dimension beyond the apprehension of man's physical senses. This dimension, or second heaven, is the heavenly place between the first and the third and is the dimension of the created spirit realm, including both angels and demons. They function in this realm hidden from human eyes, yet they enter from it into our realm as the need arises. The best scriptural example to show what is meant by this assertion can be seen in the events following the resurrection of Jesus:

> *A week later his disciples were in the house again, and Thomas was with them. Though the doors were locked, Jesus came and stood among them and said, "Peace be with you!" Then he said to Thomas, "Put your finger here; see my hands. Reach out your hand and put it into my side. Stop doubting and believe."*
> John 20:26

We have seen in Jesus the ability to move through physical barriers, such as the walls or locked doors here, while still maintaining a physical form that could be touched by Thomas. Jesus passed between the second and the first heavens and was able to do so without danger. He became flesh and let them touch him. This correlates with the angels and demons in the Old Testament (cf. Genesis 18) being able to assume human form moving from the second to the first heaven.

Elsewhere, we are told He appeared to the disciples in a

71

different form:

> *Afterward Jesus appeared in a different form*
> *to two of them while they were walking in the country.*
> *These returned and reported it to the rest;*
> *but they did not believe them either.*
> Mark 16:12

Somehow, there is a realm in which Jesus was functioning, not in the realm of the Father, but somehow closely tied to the temporal realm. In Acts 1, Jesus came out of the second heaven and was speaking to the disciples. Then He was taken into heaven (the third heaven) to commence the duties of intercessor at the right hand of the Father (cf. Romans 8:34). From that place, the third heaven, He has yet to come back and physically appear to us as He did while functioning in the second heaven.

The separation between the three heavens is best illustrated in Ephesians 4:8-10:

> *This is why it says: "When he ascended on high,*
> *he led captives in his train and gave gifts to men."*
> *(What does "he ascended" mean except that*
> *he also descended to the lower, earthly regions?*
> *He who descended is the very one who ascended higher*
> *than all the heavens, in order to fill the whole universe.)*

Having left the first heaven, or the temporal reality (His body was at this very moment in the tomb of Joseph of Aramathea), He (or His spirit) passed into the second heaven after He physically died; that is, *"He descended to the lower, earthly regions"* to the place of Sheol to preach to the captives there. He then took those redeemed into the third heaven to be with the Father and left the wicked dead in the second heaven, which is the place of the lake of fire. Passing from one heaven (reality or realm) to the other is difficult, maybe impossible. In fact, it may be impossible for the temporal to be in the third heaven at all. But spirit, whether man's spirit, angels (of Darkness or Light), or God, can pass between the three.

Many prophets and other dreamers tell of passing into the heavenlies and returning to the temporal realm. These stories are divided into two distinct types. The first kind takes the person, probably in the spirit rather than in a physical sense, into the throne room of the Father. These events are marked by one distinction: no one ever actually sees the Father:

No one has seen the Father except the one who is from God; only he has seen the Father.
John 6:46

I experienced this type of vision first in 1992 when I was in a deliverance session with a pastor. The team had been moving through our regular method of deliverance ministry for the person when, suddenly, I was transported into the throne room of the Living God. I was sitting facing a group of angels who were dancing joyously over a report concerning the person for whom we were praying. There was an angel sitting on either side of me; the one on the right had what looked like some sort of clipboard. As I looked to my right, there were huge billows of smoke and I knew Father was seated on His throne somewhere in the midst of the smoke. Then, the angels showed me what seemed to be a high-speed video of the person's life from the moment of birth to the present. It happened so fast I was unable to speak clearly beyond an, "OH!" or a "WOW!" now and then. Back in the living room where my body was, the team watched me spitting out these and other partial phrases, and wondered what had become of me. They tried to take notes, but all they got was bits and pieces of all I was seeing.

A sort of knowing rather than actual verbal message

communicated everything. Having seen the entirety of the person's life, I then knew the angel on my right was about to show me the date of the person's death and I shouted, both in the heavenlies and in the physical realm, "NO! NO! NO!" He looked up in the direction of the smoke and then stopped flipping the pages. Then I asked why this person had been subjected to so much destruction. I looked toward the smoke and suddenly Jesus leaned out of it on the right side. He looked at me with great compassion and, never saying a thing, He held up His hand showing me the scars. I knew He was saying, "So he would know me in my suffering." I began to weep as I had never wept before. Suddenly, I felt myself falling and physically thumping back into my body. I kept my eyes closed for a few moments, not wanting it to be over. But I opened my eyes and, sure enough, I was back in the living room again. I had visited the third heaven and returned alive.

The other type of heavenly vision is one into the heavenlies, but it is the realm of angels and demons. We have moved in this realm for many years. There are reports of seeing demons and angels in operation, being able to look in on their plans and schemes undetected. This is the realm where prophetic deliverance ministry takes place. Father releases us into this realm through the Spirit, so we can thwart the schemes of the Enemy and set the captives free. It is a simple operation of the prophecy, dreams, and visions guaranteed in Joel 2. There is a veil separating our sight from the realm of the spirits. This veil is the fruit of the curse pronounced upon Adam and Eve. They lost their ability to see, not only into the realm of the Father, but the realm of the spirits as well. The well-known story of the appearance of a talking snake reveals that our first parents could see the realm of angels as well as the realm of Father.

From time to time throughout the history of mankind, the veil has been penetrated and both angels and demons have appeared in human form. One obvious occurrence of angels moving into the realm of the tangible is the story of Abraham and Lot in Genesis 18. Three men appeared to Abraham, one of whom was the Lord, Himself. The other two are identified as angels. These beings took an active role in the destruction of Sodom and Gomorrah. Evil angels had the ability to appear in human form, as well:

> *The Nephilim were on the earth in those days*
> *—and also afterward—when the sons of God*
> *went to the daughters of men and had children by them.*
> *They were the heroes of old, men of renown.*
> Genesis 6:4

These beings were evil angels who took human form and produced a race of giants upon the earth. Noah's flood was sent not only to purify the earth of sin, but to eliminate these hybrids from mankind's blood lines. When the Lord chose Noah, he chose him on the basis of not being contaminated by demonic blood:

> *This is the account of Noah. Noah was a righteous man,*
> *blameless among the people of his time,*
> *and he walked with God.*
> Genesis 6:9

A careful examination of the word translated 'blameless' reveals more than his righteousness before God. It reveals the fact that the seed of demons had not corrupted his bloodline. The flood, then, was necessary to prevent demon blood to be found in the veins of the Messiah many years hence. It appears, after the flood, evil angels were restricted from their previous reproductive activities. They were relegated to chains in darkness,

75

unable to appear in human form thereafter. This is the origin of the need for evil spirits to inhabit a human to accomplish their evil mission.

Principality (KJV) or Ruler (NIV)

This is the Greek word *arche* meaning "chief, magistrate, first, or ruler" (cf. Ephesians 3:10; 6:12). Principalities are the highest, most powerful class in the hierarchy of the Satanic kingdom. They influence large groups or territories such as countries, states, cities, and maybe even churches. They are the administrators of demonic influence throughout a given territory through those demonic forces who serve under them.

When spiritual warfare is performed over a city or region, the Principality or Principalities are usually the targets of that warfare. It is important to understand the power in which this level of spirit moves. We have watched church after church attempt to take on the Principality over their particular area only to find themselves beaten down or even totally destroyed.

Again, I tell you that if two of you on earth agree about anything you ask for, it will be done for you by my Father in heaven. For where two or three come together in my name, there am I with them.
Matthew 18:19-20

This principle of agreement is the key to any spiritual warfare against this level of evil spirit. To rout a Principality, there must be agreement among denominations, churches, pastors, genders, and cultures to build the level of faith and power required.

Powers (KJV) or Authorities (NIV)

This is from the Greek word *exousia* meaning "force,

authority, jurisdiction, or strength" (cf. Matthew 24:29; Ephesians 3:10; 6:12). Powers are only in subjection to Principalities. A Power is a major demonic spirit whose primary activity is to envelop a territory with the potency of a particular type of evil. A Power infiltrates every aspect of the society and culture with its particular brand of evil. What is produced by this infiltration is the "feel" or "spirit" of a city or area. This may be noticed even when driving from one territory to another. There might be a sense of darkness in one area and another may "feel" angry. Attending a number of churches in a given city makes it very clear. Many times, although the liturgies and services are quite different, there is an identical spirit underlying all of them.

Some years ago, a group of pastors (myself included) was compelled to meet for prayer regarding the city in which we all served. Each week we came together, shared, fellowshipped, developed relationship, and prayed. After more than seven months, we felt the Lord was directing us to take action. We agreed we would return the next week, having fasted and prayed separately, with whatever name the Spirit of God spoke to our hearts. We had not discussed any names or situations; we simply waited upon Father for Him to reveal it.

We came back together the next week and followed a plan the Lord had given us. We moved through a time of praise into worship, and finally it was time to lay it on the table. Most of the participants had never walked in this kind of prophetic exercise, so there was a great sense of tension in the room. Suddenly, one of the pastors thumped a piece of paper down on the table and nearly shouted, "I think his name is Seth!" The pastor across the table from him sprang to his feet and ran screaming from the room. We all sat there with our eyes bugging out until he returned to tell us he had been given the same name. Two of the other pastors were given functions for the spirit and my father spoke what we have come to understand was his proper name in his angelic (demonic) language.

Now it was time to act.

I explained to the group that demons are not omnipresent, so we would have to call the demon to us to cast him out. As one they yelled, "NO!" Instead, we sent a lower level spirit to inform him of our attack, and we proceeded to command him and any unclean spirit under his authority to leave our spiritual territory. Although we could not see it with our physical eyes, we knew there was something happening as thousands upon thousands of demons streamed out of the area. My mother was in another part of the house praying for us, not knowing exactly what we were doing. She related afterward that, although her eyes were closed, the room became so dark she opened her eyes to see what was going on. Nothing had changed in the natural realm, so she closed them again and soon everything became very bright. For the next several years, that city experienced wonderful economic renewal. A Christian mayor was elected, area churches began to grow once again, and the general outlook of the city was strikingly positive.

A few weeks after the victory, one of the pastors came across some information pertinent to what we had done. While researching in the public library, he found a number of books by an author named Jane Roberts. Ms. Roberts had been one of the early influences in the New Age Movement relating to the area of channeling. It turned out these books were the recorded conversations with a spirit she had channeled whose name was Seth. Of course, when this information hit the group what hair we had left immediately stood on end.

The key to the victory was agreement. The makeup of the group of praying pastors included a Nazarene, a United Methodist, an Assemblies of God pastor, a renewalist, an independent Pentecostal, and one from the Christian and Missionary Alliance. This was as theologically diverse a group as one could put together, yet when we dropped our distinctives and focused upon the task to which we were called, the Lord moved greatly for that city.

Rulers (KJV) or Powers (NIV)

This is from the Greek word *kosmokrator* meaning "decorated rank, world ruler of the spiritual forces, one who tends or provides" (cf. Ephesians 6:12). Rulers appear to be the ranking members of the lower ranks of demons (cf. Eph.3: 10; 6:12). If we could put it in corporate terms, they would comprise all levels of middle management. Sometimes they call themselves a "prince." They are lesser in rank and power than Principalities or Powers. They are the leaders of the rank and file of the spiritual forces of evil. They exert evil on small groups or individuals in conjunction with the myriad of demons at their disposal.

Spiritual Wickedness in High Places (KJV) or Spiritual Forces of Evil (NIV)

These Spiritual Forces of Evil are the least powerful beings in the demonic realms. They are personal beings permeating individuals with evil (cf. Ephesians 6:12). They seem to be the foot soldiers of the Kingdom of Darkness. We generally refer to them as demons, evil spirits, or unclean spirits.

Although they are presented in Scripture as a group, they do not carry the same authority or power. In fact, they differ in varying degrees of wickedness:

*Then it goes and takes with it seven other spirits **more wicked than itself***, *and they go in and live there. And the final condition of that man is worse than the first.*
Matthew 12:45 (bold mine)

It is with this level of spirit that deliverance ministry is most concerned. The responsibility to cast (drive) them out is given to all believers.

And these signs will accompany those who believe:
*In my name they **will drive out demons**; they will speak*
in new tongues; they will pick up snakes with their
hands; and when they drink deadly poison,
it will not hurt them at all; they will place their
hands on sick people, and they will get well.
Mark 16:17 (bold mine)

Their job is to harass and influence both believers and unbelievers. They counterfeit the indwelling presence of the Holy Spirit by inhabiting the bodies and/or minds of people. They are committed to taking as many humans as possible with them into the Lake of Fire. To that end, they lie, cheat, influence, manipulate, multiply sickness and disease, and confuse anyone who will give them place.

Demonization

The phrase "demon possessed" (found in most English versions of the Bible) has been adopted in error by translators. We find, by deeper study of the language, the word "demonization" is a more accurate term. We will avoid the details of the exegesis and plunge right to the point. The participle used most often in the New Testament for the presence or power of unclean spirits is the Greek word *daimonizomai*, which means "a demon caused passivity." This definition indicates a somewhat passive individual; that is, one who by ignorance, neglect, or others-imposed trauma, allows a demonic being to exercise some sort of control in his or her life. An unclean spirit influences the person, who is passive to the demon's action to one extent or another.

80

This indicates a continuing state of being harassed by demons.

There has been much confusion caused by incorrectly translating *daimonizomenos* as "demon possessed." That is because "possession" implies ownership. But Scripture is clear, demons own nothing:

> *And he blessed him, and said, "Blessed be Abram of the most high God, **possessor of heaven and earth.** "*
> Genesis 14:19 KJV (bold mine)

They are only counterfeiting what they see the Father doing. The New Testament treats them as squatters or invaders of territory which is not their own. As invaders, demons can exercise control over only what is yielded (actively or passively) to their control:

> *Don't you know that when you offer yourselves to someone to obey him as slaves, you are slaves to the one whom you obey?*
> Romans 6:16

The faulty translation strikes fear of *ownership* rather than indicating the true aspect of *control* or *power over*. The owner of a house is much different in nature and function from a squatter who makes the house his home without the permission of the owner. The owner has legal and moral deed of ownership, while the squatter has control only while he is resident. He owns nothing in the legal or moral sense. Demons can control only the aspects of one's life, which are yielded to them. Therefore, the proper translation of *daimonizomenos* should be "under the control of, exercised by, or influenced by one or more demons, therefore: demonized."

Improper assumptions have led to confusion regarding demonization. Many have attempted to explain demon possession by creating levels of demonic possession not holding with any biblical definition. There are three main definitions that must be discarded. First is "demon possession," meaning someone who is powerless under a demon's power. A "demon-possessed" person is described as completely controlled by the demon such as a puppet is controlled by the puppeteer. We have eliminated this theory for several reasons, not the least of which is simple logic. In studying Biblical cases of deliverance, one oddity comes clear: if the person were completely controlled by the unclean spirit, why would that spirit come anywhere near Jesus? Let's examine one such case.

> *They went across the lake to the region of the Gerasenes. When Jesus got out of the boat, a man with an evil spirit came from the tombs to meet him. This man lived in the tombs, and no one could bind him any more, not even with a chain. For he had often been chained hand and foot, but he tore the chains apart and broke the irons on his feet. No one was strong enough to subdue him. Night and day among the tombs and in the hills he would cry out and cut himself with stones. When he saw Jesus from a distance, he ran and fell on his knees in front of him. He shouted at the top of his voice, "What do you want with me, Jesus, Son of the Most High God? Swear to God that you won't torture me!" For Jesus had said to him, "Come out of this man, you evil spirit!"*
> Mark 5:1-8

Here are two interesting points for this discussion. First, we find the man with an evil spirit *"came from the tombs to meet him."* Demons are highly intelligent creations of the Most High, so how foolish is this demon to come out and meet the Son of the Living God? If the man were "possessed" as some would teach, then the demon would have driven the possessed person as far from Jesus as possible.

Next, consider the fact the demon knew who Jesus was. It was not as if he came around a corner and bumped into Him by mistake. The fact is *"When he saw Jesus from a distance, he ran and fell on his knees in front of him."* It is clear the man, even at this level of demonization, had enough control over himself to run to Jesus for help. This is what we call the "coming to." There is always a "coming to" with regards to demonization. That is why we are unable to perform deliverance on anyone who is not a willing participant. The person must exercise his or her will in the "coming to" for help. The only exceptions to this rule are when the demonized person is a child or is incapable of making decisions due to mental defect or other handicap. In any of these cases, the parent or guardian of the individual must "come to" us for help.

The second level of demonic activity wrongly taught is called "demon oppression," meaning someone who is only harassed by a demon, though not completely under the demon's control.

Finally, there is "demon obsession," meaning someone who becomes an addict (any sort of addiction) or is driven by a demon in an obsessive or compulsive manner. All three of these have been taught to explain the presence of demons in or on people, yet they have no biblical basis. To be demonized is to be demonized, whether by one demon or a thousand. It is simply demonization.

After sharing my Deliverance Seminar with a group of pastors at a summer camp, it became clear this point must be made. So in the following months, we redeveloped our curriculum to deal with the question of two King James Version words. These two words provide the basis for this faulty understanding. First, is the word "oppressed," found only one time in the New Testament relating to demonic activity. That Scripture says,

> *How God anointed Jesus of Nazareth with the Holy*
> *Ghost and with power: who went about doing good,*
> *and healing all that were **oppressed** of the devil;*
> *for God was with him.*
> Acts 10:38 KJV (bold mine)

The word translated "oppressed" is *katadunasteuo*. It is defined as "to exercise dominion against." Obviously, this is not a separate level of demonization, but simply a restatement of the same idea as *daimonizomai*.

The other word is "vexed," and it is found only four times in the New Testament relating to demonic activity. Here are those verses:

> *And, behold, a woman of Canaan came out of the same*
> *coasts, and cried unto him, saying,*
> *"Have mercy on me, O Lord, thou Son of David;*
> *my daughter is grievously **vexed** with a devil."*
> Matthew 15:22 KJV (bold mine)

This is a mistranslation. The Greek word *daimonizomai* is the same word translated "demon possessed" elsewhere which we have shown to mean "demonized."

The next case:

> *Lord, have mercy on my son: for he is lunatic,*
> *and sore **vexed**: for ofttimes he falleth into the fire,*
> *and oft into the water.*
> Matthew 17:15 KJV (bold mine)

In this verse we find the Greek word *paskho*, meaning 'to be affected by or to experience.' We do not find this word means anything substantially different than *daimonizomai*.

The last two instances of the word "vexed" being used are as follows:

> *And they that were **vexed** with unclean spirits:*
> *and they were healed.*
> Luke 6:18 KJV (bold mine)

This is the Greek word *ochleo*, meaning "to mob or harass." It seems to carry the same definition as *daimonizomai* once again. The second instance of *ochleo* being translated "vexed" is this:

> *There came also a multitude out of the cities round*
> *about unto Jerusalem, bringing sick folks, and them*
> *which were **vexed** with unclean spirits:*
> *and they were healed every one.*
> Acts 5:16 KJV (bold mine)

Our conclusion is the words "oppressed" and "vexed" are not different levels of demonic activity; rather, they are simply descriptive terms meaning the same thing as *daimonizomai*.

Chapter 6

Prophetic Deliverance

Deliverance Methodology

There are plenty of methods for casting out demons, and I do not want to offend those who incorporate any methods that actually produce fruit in the people they are serving. But to be forthright, I have major concerns about many methodologies, some of the abuses connected with them, and, of course, those offering hope without the ability or power to really produce freedom. Over the years, we have had to undo a tremendous amount of faulty information about deliverance ministry, and we then minister the correct information required to produce freedom, which is the true fruit of deliverance. We have battled the imbalances of the Charismatic renewal, the physical, mental and emotional abuses which accompany so many of these types of ministries, and the ignorance and fear of the general church population concerning the joys and freedoms of legitimate deliverance ministry. We believe Prophetic Deliverance is the answer to what ails deliverance ministry in this country and around the world. We further believe Prophetic Deliverance is the answer to what ails the church in general. Now it is time to define Prophetic Deliverance, so let us lay some foundation for what it entails.

Connecting Prophecy and Deliverance

One might ask, "What is prophecy?" Prophecy, simply put, is hearing *from*, and then speaking *for* God. It is not at the level of the inspired prophetic utterance producing Scripture, but it is a release of the thoughts, precepts and heart of the Father. Paul urged us, through his writings to the Corinthians, to earnestly desire to prophesy:

> *Follow the way of love and eagerly desire spiritual*
> *gifts, especially the gift of prophecy.*
> 1 Corinthians 14:1

The Holy Spirit Gift of Prophecy is the first of two fundamental operating principles of Prophetic Deliverance. The second is flowing in the gift of Distinguishing Between Spirits.

> *To one there is given through the Spirit the message of*
> *wisdom, to another the message of knowledge by means*
> *of the same Spirit, to another faith by the same Spirit,*
> *to another gifts of healing by that one Spirit, to another*
> *miraculous powers, **to another prophecy, to another***
> ***distinguishing between spirits**, to another speaking*
> *in different kinds of tongues, and to still another the*
> *interpretation of tongues. All these are the work of one*
> *and the same Spirit, and he gives them to each one, just*
> *as he determines.*
> 1 Corinthians 12:8-11 (bold mine)

One must be accomplished in hearing the voice of the Spirit of God in order to make a determination it is indeed Him and not either one's own mind or some unclean spirit. Through prophecy, we hear the Holy Spirit's instruction and through the Gift of Discerning Between Spirits, we speak the name and function of the unclean spirit. Prophetic Deliverance, by its very definition, employs the prophetic giftings to make the diagnosis, name the demon, and to verify it has been cast out. The prophetic authority, which has been returned to the Church in these last days, has been given for the use of the Body of Christ in every aspect of ministry. Joel 2 reveals the nature of this ministry:

And afterward, I will pour out my Spirit on all people.
Your sons and daughters will prophesy, your old men
shall dream dreams, your young men shall see visions.
Even on my servants, both men and women, I will pour
out my Spirit in those days.
Joel 2:28-29

It is clear in these last days the primary operational gift of the rank and file will be prophecy; it will be hearing from and speaking for the Living God. Dreams, visions, and prophecy incorporate the same characteristics of hearing from God and transmitting that information to others. When Peter preached during the first few hours after the Church age was inaugurated, he was specific that this new entity upon the earth, the Church, was now and forever the fulfillment of Joel's prophecy.

So, then, Prophetic Deliverance is dependent upon the last days Gift of Prophecy.

Comparing and Contrasting Prophetic Deliverance

Of all the deliverance methods I have studied over the years, the most effective and least strenuous is Prophetic Deliverance. Almost all the other methods employed by the Church throughout its two-thousand-year history have relied upon clues and evidence, which are determined through natural means. This

88

is not to say all other deliverance methods are an operation of the flesh, exactly, but it is to say at least their method of diagnosis is suspect. A good example is the rite of exorcism practiced by the Roman Catholic Church. Although rare, this rite is still alive out of the sheer necessity of dealing with severely demonized people who are connected with the Church. In my limited experience with this type of deliverance, I have found it is seldom effective, while being incredibly demanding both upon those who perform it and upon the demonized person. The diagnosis is made through natural observation of the excessive manifestations of the evil spirit through the person. The rite involves speaking to and hearing from the demon, along with much shouting and demonstrations of what I would call natural power and authority. This so-called authority is exercised through pressing the crucifix into the flesh of the person, restraining him or her with straps, wetting the flesh with holy water, and other outward acts.

Those exorcisms I have witnessed have been characterized by long hours of arguing with or shouting at the unclean spirit and the rather violent response of the client. Eventually, it is my opinion the person is so exhausted the demon simply quiets down its manifestations so success can be declared. While I stop short of completely dismissing the rite of exorcism, I do question its validity in truly setting anyone free for the long term. The fruit we have seen is short-lived, and eventually the person moves into a sort of deadened state of living. Again, there may be exceptions, but we have not witnessed them.

Moving over into the Protestant camp, we find a variety of deliverance methods employed. First, let's examine the methods which utilize long lists of names of spirits which are called out one after the other until the ministers are satisfied the demons are gone. These lists of demons are based upon the experience of the deliverance minister or some resource he or she has developed. Some then just read over the lists until there is a reaction from the demonized person. Others examine the clues found in the natural to determine which of the demons on the list are present, and they go about casting out a spirit relating to that outward sign. A good example might be a person who is losing a fight with his temper. Anger, which is the outward, natural sign witnessed by the deliverance ministers, is named as the culprit spirit and commanded to depart. Our experience has shown that much of what can be witnessed by a cursory examination is a symptom rather than the source of the problem.

Another type of diagnostic process employs a list of interview questions helping the minister determine the names and functions of the resident demons. This is only an exercise in the psychological and, many times, misses the true spiritual issue facing the seeker. The interview will reveal only what the seeker is able to understand and expose, while in the majority of cases, the person is merely aware of the outward physical, or inward mental product of the spirit. Let me explain what I mean. We have ministered deliverance to hundreds of people whose issues boiled down to one thing: anger. Their conclusion then is that a spirit of anger has demonized them. If we relied upon an interview, that is the only conclusion we would have been able to draw, and it would have been wrong. However, by use of the prophetic in the session, we might hear the Spirit say the source is a control spirit, or even a spirit of fear, the outward effect of which is anger.

Control spirits, which we will deal with in detail later on, are many times misdiagnosed as spirits of anger because people's response to any sort of authority issue is to get angry. When my wife went through deliverance the first time, a spirit of anger was commanded to leave. The folks who were praying for her knew her fairly well and knew she dealt with anger. They made their commands, she felt better from all the crying at the altar, and they testified of the victory. The reality of the matter was, when she went through Prophetic Deliverance several years later, it was discovered she was under the influence of a Jezebelian spirit and her anger was just a symptom of that spirit. The victory was then real and the fruit was lasting.

Avoiding Natural Understanding

When operating in Prophetic Deliverance, we avoid those things that tend to lead us by the natural understanding of the human mind and move only when the Holy Spirit relays the information to us. In this setting, our minds are not clouded by the information we have about people because we do not talk to them about their issues prior to the session. Once in the session, we seldom ask questions because it provides too much space for speculation out of what we hear, our experience, knowledge, or wisdom. The people come to us for help, but they do not need to hear from us; they need to hear from the Holy Spirit. Therefore, anything we know in the natural is a hindrance to hearing what the Spirit is saying. Once we know something by natural means, we are forced to redouble our efforts to *"take every thought into captivity"* (2 Corinthians 10:5) so we do not move on our assumptions about their issue. The more we know about a client, the harder it is to be sure we are hearing from the Holy Spirit. It can be done, but it is more difficult.

Who Is In Charge?

We have studied a number of deliverance methods where the demons seem to be in charge of the session. The ministers spend their time making demands upon unclean spirits, demanding they speak their names and reveal their identities to the deliverance team. The problem with asking a demon anything is that he is the minion of one who is the father of lies, and is therefore nearly incapable of telling the truth. Jesus' words to us are clear on this point:

91

*You belong to your father, the devil, and you want
to carry out your father's desire. He was a murderer
from the beginning, not holding to the truth, for there
is no truth in him. When he lies, he speaks his native
language, for he is a liar and the father of lies.*
John 8:44

The native language of demons is lies, so how can you expect them to tell the truth? This process is like a battle royal between the deliverance team and the demon, and the poor seeker is crushed and abused in the process. I recently heard a man tell stories about how he speaks to the demons and commands them to tell the truth. He is sure they then must tell the truth. All I could say was he is spending time talking to the wrong spirit. We are the Lord's sheep and the sheep are predisposed to hear His voice:

*I tell you the truth, the man who does not enter the
sheep pen by the gate, but climbs in by some other way,
is a thief and a robber. The man who enters by the gate
is the shepherd of his sheep. The watchman opens the
gate for him, and the sheep listen to his voice. He calls
his own sheep by name and leads them out. When he
has brought out all his own, he goes on ahead of them,
and his sheep follow him because they know his voice.
But they will never follow a stranger; in fact, they will
run away from him because they do not
recognize a stranger's voice.*
John 10:1-5

Why would someone put more stock in what a demon says, truth or not, than in what the Spirit of the Living God says? Any spirit's voice other than the Holy Spirit is a stranger's voice. This man's theological background did not make room for the prophetic, but, as silly as it seems, it made room for hearing from demons. At this point, I would urge the reader whose doctrine leaves no room for the prophetic to search the Scriptures and to evaluate such absurdity in the light of His Word.

Prophetic Deliverance differs from any other method in that we are dependent not upon the person and his or her ability to adequately articulate the issues, nor upon the demon, whose only means of communication is lies, but upon the only One unable to lie, upon the only One who speaks specifically to the heart of an issue He sees with absolute clarity. If He does not speak to an issue, so we do not speak to it. We do not probe, interview, or interrogate. We do not base our diagnosis upon what we have learned in previous sessions. We never know, going into a session, what or whom we will encounter. Therefore, our only means of truth is the voice of the Lord Himself.

We are dependent upon Him alone.

The Problems of Dependency

Having participated in more than a few thousand deliverance sessions, we have accumulated a massive amount of experience. This experience is helpful in teaching others how to do deliverance. It is also helpful when explaining what deliverance is and what it does. However, that experience itself can be a hindrance during the session. As we train deliverance teams, we find the same thing over and over: people see something they recognize from another session and they jump to the conclusion that either the same spirit is present, or the same issue is present. It makes it simple; it makes it easy; we have seen this before, so it must be the same thing again. The more one grows in experience, the more work it is to ensure that experience does not dictate our actions. Experience in the natural can greatly reduce the effectiveness in the prophetic, so one problem with this level of dependency upon the Holy Spirit is relying upon experience we have accumulated.

Another problem of operating at this level of dependency is too much information. The most difficult sessions we have ever encountered have been in taking family members through deliverance. It is often extremely difficult to separate what one already knows in the natural from what the Spirit of God is speaking. The result, many times, is unwanted manifestations, lessened authority, or some other disaster.

Once we were serving a family member in deliverance with a team made up entirely of family members. The session was not going well, so the other three members of my team sat there with their eyes closed, straining to separate what they knew in the natural about this person and what the Holy Spirit was saying. The unclean spirit saw I was not being guarded, so he came out of the client and began to physically squeeze me. As my breath was compressed out of my lungs, I was unable to speak or make any noise to get the team's attention. I can still hear the vertebrae of my spine popping as he squeezed me tighter and tighter. After several terrifying minutes, one of the team members opened his eyes and saw what was happening, took authority over the spirit, and I was released. The interesting part was trying to explain it to our doctor the next day while he was trying to get me put back together.

The same problem can be found in the everyday function of prophecy. For example, if you know in the natural that the person to whom you are prophesying is about to receive some sort of blessing and the Holy Spirit speaks it to you as well, it makes it difficult to know whether the word came by natural means or by the Spirit. That is why we teach prophetic people to be sure not to claim absolute authority when prophesying. This can be done simply by using the words, "I think this what the Spirit is saying" or by using some other disclaimer. Phrases to be avoided are anything like, "Thus saith the Lord" or some other definitive term. If you say "this is what the Lord is saying" for sure, then the word must be completely accurate. Otherwise, there must be some room left for the flesh to sneak into the prophecy; after all, *"...we know in part and we prophesy in part"* (1 Corinthians 13:9).

Therefore, the best we can hope for in the prophetic is *part*. People always bleed some of their own thoughts, ideas, impressions, and experience into what might otherwise be a helpful, powerful prophecy. While we must create as complete a dependency upon the voice of the Lord as possible, it is obvious even to me that error cannot be avoided entirely. Deliverance ministers and prophets alike must be made aware of the problem and work hard at ensuring whose voice they are hearing, whether it is their own, the voice of an unclean spirit, or the voice of the Good Shepherd Himself.

Paul's further instruction takes care of it:

*Two or three prophets should speak, and the others should **weigh carefully** what is said.*
1 Corinthians 14:29 (bold mine)

*Do not put out the Spirit's fire; do not treat prophecies with contempt. **Test everything**. Hold on to the good. Avoid every kind of evil.*
1 Thessalonians 5:19-22 (bold mine)

Testing Prophetic Word

All prophetic word must be put to the test. We compare it with eating fish: you pick out the good meat and you throw away the bones, the scales, and the other inedible parts. We are not shy in doing it for our bellies, why are we so tentative in doing it for our spirits? In deliverance ministry, we separate the meat from the bones through the use of the scriptural principle of two or three witnesses:

> *A matter must be established by the*
> *testimony of two or three witnesses.*
> Deuteronomy 19:15b

We do that by not speaking out what we think the Holy Spirit is saying. Instead, we write it down so complete integrity is maintained. Early on in our ministry we found if someone says, "Thus and so," the other people present may be inclined to agree and say they have the same thing. It is not that they were liars. It's just the natural fear of being wrong might overwhelm us and make us say, "I had that, too" when we had something entirely different. In the section on our method later in the book, we will see the how this confirmation process works.

Prophetic Deliverance

Prophetic Deliverance is the easiest method for casting out demons. There is no lengthy screening process, no long list of interview questions, just a few people gathered to hear what Father has to say concerning the client's spiritual state. Although a high level of prophetic anointing is present in all deliverance sessions, the Holy Spirit is careful to reveal only what is necessary for the task to be completed. We are not there to affirm someone's call, tell him to move to Timbuktu and become a missionary, help him find the set of lost keys, tell him what his mate looks like, or any other prophetic act. The Holy Spirit reveals exactly what we need to know, no more, no less. The result is a very efficient method for personal deliverance. The time has been pared down from three to four hours to around fifteen minutes. As we will see later on, the second portion of the session deals with the brokenhearted and the crushed in spirit, and that takes much more time.

Other methods we have studied take a tremendous amount

of time. One gentleman's process takes between six and eight hours. He recommends a large team—fifteen or twenty people—and they sit around and sing hymns at the demons, and read Scripture at them while the leader demands the demons speak through the person. Sometimes they do not get done on the first session and must come back together to do it all over again the next day. This kind of strain is abusive to the client. After all, the demon has abused him enough, and we are here to eliminate abuse. Why are we multiplying the strain? Prophetic Deliverance is designed to release the person from his chains, not to beat him up for hours and abuse him more.

Our teams are trained to speak to the client when they come in, greeting them and chatting, but from that point on in the session, we converse only with the Holy Spirit. When it is time to cast out the unclean spirit[s], we speak directly to the demon by the name[s] we have diagnosed and tell it to leave. The client's job in the session is to pay attention and stand in agreement with what is being said. It all seems like a quiet little prayer meeting. There are no manifestations—we do not allow them—there is just powerful deliverance from the influence of unclean spirits.

Fasting and Prayer

The ministry of deliverance, then, must be an act of the prophetic rather than an act of logic or psychology. We are not interested in great experience, psychological training, or wonderful information. We are interested in hearing what the Holy Spirit has to say. That focus makes the preparation for deliverance very simple: be in contact with the Father. Practice being in the presence of the Lord and hearing His voice. We recommend a lifestyle of fasting and prayer to facilitate this intimacy with Father. Jesus was clear when He was challenged about His higher level of authority in deliverance. He said,

Then came the disciples to Jesus apart,
and said, "Why could not we cast him out?"
And Jesus said unto them, "Because of your unbelief:
for verily I say unto you, If ye have faith as a grain of
mustard seed, ye shall say unto this mountain,
Remove hence to yonder place; and it shall remove;
and nothing shall be impossible unto you. Howbeit this
kind goeth not out but by prayer and fasting."
Matthew 17:19-21

His answer does not imply you could fast and pray once just to rout this certain type of unclean spirit. Rather, His thought was that a lifestyle of fasting and prayer is the foundation for higher levels of authority against the unclean realm. Once one is established in this kind of lifestyle, the authority for any level of wickedness is available. This takes us to the next topic of discussion concerning deliverance ministry: spiritual authority. In the next chapter, we will examine the role of spiritual authority in deliverance ministry.

Chapter 7

Spiritual Authority

The Hierarchy of Life

Father has established levels of authority in every aspect of life on earth. In the animal kingdom the young males are in continual war with the older males for domination of the herd. In the food chain, the bugs eat the smaller bugs that have eaten some sort of plant life, and are in turn eaten by large animals and fish. Soon, the fish are eaten by bigger and bigger fish, and they are eaten by land-based predators. There is a hierarchy of life on this planet.

The same is true of life in the spirit realm. The angels were created and placed in a hierarchy. We find this hierarchy presented in several places in Scripture. The most notable is in Ephesians:

For we wrestle not against flesh and blood,
but against principalities, against powers,
against the rulers of the darkness of this world,
against spiritual wickedness in high places.
Ephesians 6:12

What we find is a progression of rank from the highest to the least. There are principalities, then powers, then rulers, then spiritual forces of evil, or the rank and file of demonic beings. Each level of angelic being, both good and evil, is subject to another higher level of authority.

Corporate Hierarchy

In the corporate world, there is a hierarchy called the corporate ladder. When one is employed by a company, he must start at the lowest rungs of the hierarchy. His life is henceforth consumed by moving up the ladder, taking the position of the person above him, until he reaches the top, or at least as close to the top as possible. Just like the hierarchy in the animal kingdom, this hierarchy creates a natural competition to step on or over the person who stands in the way of our progress. Many corporate ladders more closely resemble the food chain (it's a dog-eat-dog world) than a corporate institution. Each person in the corporation knows who is next in line for promotion, whom they can command, and whom they must serve. With each promotion, there are fewer people above them and more below, and that's the way we like it.

Military Hierarchy

The day I arrived at Lakeland Air Force Base in San Antonio, Texas, was the day I began my most frightening crash course on hierarchal authority. Before we even got out of the bus from the airport, some obviously insane man in blue clothes began screaming obscenities at us. Who did he think he was talking to me like that? Did he not understand we had been in the air for hours and we were tired from the long flight? What soon became clear was that this lunatic now *owned* me. He could tell me where to go, come crashing into my bedroom (which I shared with fifty other guys) at any time of the day or night beating on a garbage can or screaming at the top of his lungs and, most horrible of all, he could send me to jail if I talked back to him about his actions.

The military is the final stop on the trail of hierarchal organizations. Every person in the military is quite aware where he fits in the scope of authority. Unlike the corporate hierarchy, in the military one's position is plainly displayed on one's clothing. So when speaking to another member of the military, it is abundantly clear which person has authority over the other. When I had two stripes on my shirtsleeve, I was at the mercy of everyone who had more than two stripes on his. It was a glorious day when I sewed on my stripes indicating I was now a Staff Sergeant. When something had to be done, I was now responsible, but at least I could tell a lot more people what to do.

The command structure in the military was created for a reason: when something needs to be done, it is important to know who is in charge. When an officer makes a demand (they call them commands) upon your person, you do not have the option of questioning him; you simply do what he says. In a combat situation, it is vital the soldiers work in concert with one another. If there is no one in charge or, worse yet, if decisions are made by committee, people die. Forceful, competent leadership is the key to any battle and the survival of the soldiers.

Old Testament Hierarchy

One reflection of God's plan for a hierarchy among His people can be found in the account of Moses and the Children of Israel. Moses was sent by God to lead the Israelites out of Egypt, and he, after a few plagues, found himself in the middle of the desert worn out by the daily task of settling disputes among the people. This is where his father-in-law Jethro spoke the word of the Lord to him:

101

> *But select capable men from all the people—men*
> *who fear God, trustworthy men who hate dishonest*
> *gain—and appoint them as officials over thousands,*
> *hundreds, fifties and tens. Have them serve as judges*
> *for the people at all times, but have them bring every*
> *difficult case to you; the simple cases they can decide*
> *themselves. That will make your load lighter,*
> *because they will share it with you.*
> Exodus 18:21-22

So from that moment, all Israelites knew there were officials over themselves and nine others, over themselves and forty-nine others, over themselves and ninety-nine others, and over themselves and nine hundred and ninety-nine others. At the top of that pyramid of power sat Moses. The only cases coming to him were those that could not be settled by the officials below him in the hierarchy. Moses was in charge before the Lord, and the officials served God and Moses by commanding the people. This plan was the desire of the Father's heart for His people. He alone would govern them through a series of levels of authority who could be trusted to know and do His will. This type of government is called a "theocracy," that is, governed by God.

New Testament Hierarchy

When Jesus appeared on the earth, He clarified the picture of the Divine hierarchy. It began with a discussion He had with His disciples about authority:

> *Jesus called them together and said, "You know that*
> *those who are regarded as rulers of the Gentiles lord*
> *it over them, and their high officials exercise authority*
> *over them. Not so with you. Instead, whoever wants to*

become great among you must be your servant, and
whoever wants to be first must be slave of all. For even
the Son of Man did not come to be served, but to serve,
and to give his life as a ransom for many."
Mark 10:42-45

Jesus cut right to the heart of the matter: there is a powerful difference between the first three types of hierarchy and the hierarchy of the Kingdom of God. That difference lies in the direction of progression. In the animal kingdom, power is exercised from the higher to the lesser. The same is true of the corporate ladder. In the military, the higher echelons have absolute authority over those under them, and they rule from the top down. In each of these hierarchies, the higher levels have the authority and the ability to enforce their demands. But look at what Jesus has said: *"whoever wants to become great among you must be your servant, and whoever wants to be first must be slave of all."* To be the great one in this new Kingdom requires taking a position of servanthood.

Imagine it: *servanthood*!

Instead of exercising authority down the chain of command from a lofty position of power, the exact opposite is true: authority flows from *below*. What is even more perplexing is that it is relational authority. A servant has no power to enforce his demands upon the people. Obedience to a servant's authority is based upon his relationship with the people he governs and their choice to comply. Biblical submission is dependent upon whether the parties agree, under God, to submit to one another. Therefore, the relationship becomes the centerpiece of the authority structure. Once a trusting relationship is built, the authority can be exercised within the structure of that relationship.

Rank and Function

Take a breath here and stay sharp. If you miss this, you will be completely ineffective as a deliverance minister. Each person who is born anew into the Kingdom of God gains the same rank: child of God. We are all His children—no more, no less. He does not love one of His children more than the other; He is not more pleased with you than He is with someone else. In fact, He sees us as one and the same, His children:

> *Then Peter began to speak: "I now realize how true it is that **God does not show favoritism** but accepts men from every nation who fear him and do what is right."*
> Acts 10:34 (bold mine)

This has been established, to Father we all have the same rank: child. Therefore, one is not better than the other. Once it has been understood we all have the same rank, we can investigate the areas of separation, which are evident within the Body of Christ. These distinctions have to do with the governmental hierarchy of the Kingdom of God. Each person functions with different giftings, talents, burdens, visions, and anointing.

> *There are different kinds of gifts, but the same Spirit. There are different kinds of service, but the same Lord. There are different kinds of working, but the same God works all of them in all men.*
> 1 Corinthians 12:4-6

> *And in the church God has appointed first of all apostles, second prophets, third teachers, then workers of miracles, also those having gifts of healing, those able to help others, those with gifts of administration,*

104

*and those speaking in different kinds of tongues. Are
all apostles? Are all prophets? Are all teachers? Do
all work miracles? Do all have gifts of healing? Do all
speak in tongues? Do all interpret?*
1 Corinthians 12:28-30

With the influence of our former way of thinking, it is easy to
distort this into a corporate structure where authority and power
reside in the higher levels of the ladder. But is it not to be so
with us.

The Inverted Pyramid

As opposed to the ways of the corporate world, authority in
the Kingdom of God resides below and flows up from the place
of servanthood. We call this the Inverted Pyramid. We've all
heard of pyramid schemes where those in the lower tiers work
and the profit makes its way up the pyramid to the top person.
With our pyramid, the reverse is true.

Here is a sketch to make it a little clearer:

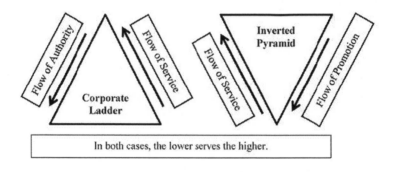

In both cases, the lower serves the higher.

*Be devoted to one another in brotherly love.
Honor one another above yourselves.*
Romans 12:10

The ways of the corporate world have so infected our thinking within the Body of Christ that the Church has become a corporate entity, with our leadership scrambling to make it just a little better than the church down the street, or to personally get elected to some District office or another. This is not what Jesus intended when He left His disciples here to birth the Church. His heart is for servanthood, not in exercising domination over the lower ranks of parishioners. We have spent much time counseling and deprogramming people who have been subjected to this kind of spiritual abuse in the Church. Apparently, pastors and other leaders make it clear the rank and file, the average pew-warming Christian, exists to serve the leadership. They impose their personal paradigms of marriage (often choosing whom one can marry), child rearing, education, family life, work life, and leisure time.

If you are in such a church right now, get out immediately! Spiritual authority exists to serve, not to make you a slave to the whims of the leadership. This is especially true of many independent churches where there is no outside authority influencing the leadership. If your leadership is not serving from below, they are out of the proper order of spiritual authority.

Serving from Below

What does 'serving from below' mean? Paul makes it quite clear in his letter to the Church at Ephesus:

> *It was he who gave some to be apostles, some to be prophets, some to be evangelists, and some to be pastors and teachers, to prepare God's people for works of service, so that the body of Christ may be built up until we all reach unity in the faith and in the knowledge of the Son of God and become mature,*

attaining to the whole measure of the fullness of Christ.
Ephesians 4:11-13

The God-given leadership of the Church exists to equip the people of God to do works of service. It is our job to train, equip and prepare the rank and file to do great exploits for the Kingdom. Somehow it has been turned upside down so the average Church person exists to make the leader appear to be great, to serve his or her vision, and to sit quietly in the pew while the superstar shows off before the congregation. The best image of this is the evident attitude of many of the ministers seen on television who are in business to get money from the people to build their vast empires. It stands opposed to the servant attitude of many who, like the late Mother Theresa, gave her life for the lost and the lowly of India, serving (ministering) from below.

Servanthood is a very easy word to say, but it most difficult to live when all of our natural instincts demand we be noticed, we be promoted, and we gain recognition for our accomplishments. Some of the greatest servants of the Most High serve in small places in anonymity, never making the news or getting a pat on the back. I am convinced Jesus was serious when He said,

Not so with you. Instead, whoever wants to become great among you must be your servant, and whoever wants to be first must be your slave—just as the Son of Man did not come to be served, but to serve, and to give his life as a ransom for many.
Matthew 20:26-28

It is the job of the leadership to make those above them greater than they, much as a parent's desire to see their child succeed and fulfill their life's purpose.

Authority and Deliverance Ministry

Pastor Fred called me looking for help with one of his people. He and several others had spent the past few nights sitting up with one of his parishioners who kept throwing fits, cutting herself with knives, and otherwise appearing to have completely lost her mind. They had taken her to the hospital to make sure nothing physical was the issue and were told "it is all in her head." He had called another pastor in his area to help, and a team arrived that evening armed with Bibles and a shofar. They prayed and commanded, yelled and demanded, and they even blew the shofar in the woman's ear. The poor woman not only did not get better, she even seemed to get worse.

Out of desperation and sheer exhaustion, Pastor Fred called me to come and see what I could do. We walked into this woman's house to find Pastor Fred and two women from his church sitting there staring off into space, with bags under their eyes, worn out from having been at war with the demon for a week as well as all night long the night before. At the beginning of the session, the demonized woman (we'll call her Sally) began to twitch. Pastor Fred told us this was always the indication when a violent manifestation had begun. So, without even thinking about it, I pointed my finger at Sally and said, "No." The twitches stopped. We continued our discussion with the pastor and his people concerning what they had been going through, and Sally twitched again and again I simply told her, "No." Within half an hour, we had cast a series of demonic beings out of Sally and she appeared to be in her right mind.

Over the course of her recovery with a local counselor, we met with her on several occasions and helped her through some other issues. It turned out she had been subjected to Satanic Ritual Abuse from the time of her birth and was suffering from Dissociative Identity Disorder (which used to be called Multiple Personality Disorder). She had been subjected to the abuse of more than three hundred personalities, each one driving her closer to self-destruction. As the demonic influence was removed, the personalities merged, one after another. Now she is able to receive the help and counsel of wise Christian counselors and work toward wholeness.

It appeared this was a point of differing levels of authority. Pastor Fred had been in the ministry longer than I; he had experience in all kinds of ecclesiastical situations, but he seemingly had no authority over what was happening to Sally. When I was able to simply say, "No" and the demon obeyed me, it made Pastor Fred angry. He asked me what in the world had happened, so I explained it to him. Technically, there are no levels of authority. There are only levels of faith. We can see it more clearly from this biblical example:

> *When they came to the crowd, a man approached Jesus and knelt before him. "Lord, have mercy on my son," he said. "He has seizures and is suffering greatly. He often falls into the fire or into the water. I brought him to your disciples, but they could not heal him." "O unbelieving and perverse generation," Jesus replied, "how long shall I stay with you? How long shall I put up with you? Bring the boy here to me." Jesus rebuked the demon, and it came out of the boy, and he was healed from that moment. Then the disciples came to Jesus in private and asked, "Why couldn't we drive it out?" He replied, "Because you have so little faith. I tell you the truth, if you have faith as small as a mustard seed, you can say to this mountain, 'Move from here to there' and it will move. Nothing will be impossible for you."*
> Matthew 17:14-20

If it were a matter of levels of authority, then the disciples could have cast the demon out. They had previously been given all the authority they needed when Jesus sent out the twelve and then when He sent out the seventy (or seventy-two). At that time, the specific authority was imparted to deal with demonic powers:

> *These twelve Jesus sent out with the following instructions: "Do not go among the Gentiles or enter any town of the Samaritans. Go rather to the lost sheep of Israel. As you go, preach this message: 'The kingdom of heaven is near.' Heal the sick, raise the dead, cleanse those who have leprosy, **drive out demons.** Freely you have received, freely give.*
> Matthew 10:5-8 (bold mine)

So why, all of a sudden, did they seemingly lose their authority over demons? Look closely at Jesus reaction to the father's request concerning his son. First, He uses the word "unbelieving."

> *"O unbelieving and perverse generation,"*
> *Jesus replied, ...*

Unbelief does not connect with authority. It connects with *faith.* Let's examine His explanation to the disciples when they asked Him why they couldn't cast it out.

> *He* [Jesus] *replied, "Because you have so little faith."*

The reason Pastor Fred could not cast the demons out of Sally was because his faith had not been built in the area of deliverance. Did he have the authority? Absolutely. Jesus confirms it to us in Matthew 28.

Then Jesus came to them and said, "All authority in heaven and on earth has been given to me. Therefore go and make disciples of all nations, baptizing them in the name of the Father and of the Son and of the Holy Spirit, and teaching them to obey everything I have commanded you. And surely I am with you always, to the very end of the age."
Matthew 28:18-30

All authority had been given back to Jesus, and He is the Head of the Body, the church.

And he is the head of the body, the church; *he is the beginning and the firstborn from among the dead, so that in everything he might have the supremacy.*
Colossians 1:18 (bold mine)

All of the authority of the Head must flow through the Body. If the Head of the Body has been given all authority, it is only logical all authority flows throughout the entire Body. Therefore, we are quite naturally, as parts of the Body of Christ, endued with this same authority.

O, You of Little Faith

So, the answer to Pastor Fred's dilemma lies not in the lack of authority, but in the lack of faith. Although we are given a measure of faith (Romans 12:3), we also know our faith must grow in a specific area. The way faith grows is through adversity. I once heard John Wimber speak concerning his authority in the area of healing ministry. He told how, at the beginning, everyone he prayed for seemed to either get sicker or would die. He fought the temptation to quit and finally began seeing real miracles happen through his prayers.

The same is true for deliverance ministry. The early years are, more than likely, going to be full of manifestations and failures. I know early on, we had little evident authority. We commanded the demons to be quiet, and they spoke more. We commanded the demons not to move, and they threw people and objects around the room. But, in persevering through the failure, we found the authority seemed to increase. Now, we are convinced deliverance *will* occur. Is it a matter of confidence in our ability or experience? No. It is a complete confidence in Jesus as the Deliverer. The act of faith is very simply the act of getting our mind and emotions out of the way so He can do through us, His Body, exactly what He did with His physical body during His earthly ministry. Whatever He did in that body, He can and will do through His Body, the Church. We need only get the unbelieving portions of our minds renewed to the point where we believe. Out of that belief emanates the miracle-working power to:

Heal the sick, raise the dead, cleanse
*those who have leprosy, **drive out demons**.*
Matthew 10:8 (bold mine)

Chapter 8

The Battlefield of Spiritual Warfare

It's All in Your Mind

Spiritual warfare is focused almost entirely upon the battlefield of the soul (the mind, will, and emotions).

> *For though we live in the world, we do not wage war as the world does. The weapons we fight with are not the weapons of the world. On the contrary, they have divine power to demolish strongholds. We demolish arguments and every pretension that sets itself up against the knowledge of God, and we take captive every thought to make it obedient to Christ.*
> 2 Corinthians 10:3-5

The territorial spirits have nothing on their smaller, but more deadly counterparts in trying to gain access to our thought life. The onslaught of the Enemy is focused here, so here is where we need our first line of defense. His work through territorial spirits pales in comparison to these demonic forces, simply because of the overwhelming number involved. Only when the spiritual forces of evil are thriving in individuals can the work of the Principalities succeed.

How does it all work? The Enemy and his troops are persistent in getting thoughts through our defenses undetected and into our minds. There, the thoughts are either stopped and examined, or allowed to mill around making trouble. Once a particular thought is allowed to take root, others of the same kind are easier to get though. Soon, many are piled up and are exerting control over the mind.

As this pile of thoughts gets organized, they form what Scripture calls a "stronghold." A stronghold is best understood when compared to a brick wall. Each brick represents a *thought* which enters one's mind (in spite of the source). It begins as a single brick, but with time and the influx of additional bricks, a pile is developed. Once enough bricks are put into place, the pile takes shape and becomes a wall, an impenetrable stronghold. Thoughts along the same line create a belief system (pile) and the stronghold (wall) is developed.

Let's say we entertain a thought of fear. Something happens which creates the atmosphere of fear. For example, there might be an unfamiliar *thump* one night while you are home alone. Fear. The first thought is fear. The second and third thoughts come rushing in, and soon we know for sure, although we haven't moved from the spot in which we froze when we heard the sound, there is an intruder in the house. The thoughts escalate. There is another *thump*, and we know we are about to die.

Now, a question: Have we sinned by thinking these thoughts? Scripturally speaking where do we stand?

> *For God hath not given us the spirit of fear; but of*
> *power, and of love, and of a sound mind.*
> 2 Timothy 1:7 KJV

For ye have not received the
spirit of bondage again to fear.
Romans 8:15 KJV

Fear itself is a normal human reaction to the unknown. To have a fearful thought is not sin, in and of itself. What is being said in these Scriptures implies more of a lifestyle of fear, which is in direct disobedience to the Word. That lifestyle is developed over time and most likely began through childhood experiences. Demons see the fertile ground of fear and enter to demonize the person to keep him subject to fear. So, as the darkness of fear grows, you can pretty much expect an evil spirit showing up to influence the situation.

So, the first battle is against the natural mind. Once that has been compromised, the stronghold is under construction. We increasingly relinquish control of our mind to the fear until our very existence comes under its influence. Fear rules our mind. Fear rules our relationships. Fear rules our paradigms. Fear rules our life.

Jane was the wife of a very successful radio personality. She was beautiful, had a charismatic personality and a wonderful sense of humor. She had given her life to the Lord and had walked with Him for a number of years, though it was a bumpy, unrewarding relationship. Jane's life before Christ had been ruled by fear. She was scared of everything and everybody, but once she came to Christ she thought her life of fear was over. Her expectation was that she was a new creation and the fear came under the dominion of her new Lord. But as the years wore on, it became clear, although she was truly born again, fear was still ruling her. By the time she asked for help, she was unable to leave her house. She was too afraid to drive. She could not be in crowds of people. She was virtually a prisoner in her own home.

As soon as the session began, we could see the problem. What looked like a huge bat-like creature was standing directly behind Jane, wings folded forward around her shoulders. She was completely trapped. When I spoke to the spirit of fear, he physically slid Jane four or five feet in the direction of the door. We quickly moved one of the team members between her and the door, and commanded to cease manifesting. Jane was weeping, terrified. After some probing, the Holy Spirit revealed the source of the fear, and we were able to cast him away. That very day, Jane was able to return to a normal life and progressed nicely in her walk with the Lord. The stronghold of fear housing the unclean spirits was broken and she was free.

Some Discipline Each Day Keeps the Demons Away

It's a four-letter word, isn't it? Discipline. Yet without discipline, our minds are open to all sorts of influences. Strongholds grow without impediment, and we reap the "benefits" of demonic rulership. The prevention of creating a stronghold requires discipline. It doesn't take a rocket scientist. It takes dedication to keeping the mind clear of influences other than our King.

A few simple but effective steps keep thoughts from sneaking in. First, *"be self-controlled and alert. Your enemy the devil prowls around like a roaring lion looking for someone to devour"* (1 Peter 5:8). What does it mean? Our minds are constantly bombarded with input of all kinds. Newspapers, magazines, books, television, radio, the Internet, comic books, video games, and a thousand other sources of information fill our lives. Never before has there been such a glut of information available to the general population. We input gigabytes of it every day without batting an eyelash.

This is the beginning of spiritual warfare. *"Be self-controlled and alert;"* you are being stalked. As the old saying goes, "Just because you are paranoid doesn't mean someone *isn't* following you." If you will not control the input, the input will control you.

So how does the first level of spiritual warfare work? Imagine a policeman or a security guard. Here comes an uninvited person toward the entrance of the facility you are assigned to guard. Just like that cop, HALT the thought as it comes into your mind. Keep your mind alert to the schemes of the enemy. He is very good at his job; he's had thousands of years to practice! When the thought comes, recognize it and take time to examine it to determine whether you should admit it.

Then, SEARCH the thought for its origin and its purpose:

Finally, brothers, whatever is true, whatever is noble, whatever is right, whatever is pure, whatever is lovely, whatever is admirable—if anything is excellent or praiseworthy—think about such things.
Philippians 4:8

If the thought is acceptable, then *"think on these things."* If its source cannot be determined, or if it is clearly in violation to the Word, take it CAPTIVE to Jesus Christ so its power may be broken. This is accomplished by simply praying, "Jesus, I give this thought to you. If it is from you, bring it back to me. If not, then please take it away." That is the final step, making it OBEDIENT to Christ. Submit it to Him by asking Him to take it from you as many times as necessary.

Early on, this process may seem time-consuming and bulky. But with practice, you will be able to determine the source of the thought very quickly. The practice of *"taking every thought into captivity"* is the true definition of *"liv*[ing] *by the Spirit, and you will not gratify the desires of the sinful nature"* (Galatians 5:16). It becomes part of the regenerated nature to search out

117

everything attempting entry into our minds. Every time a thought is thwarted in its attempt, another potential stronghold is averted. When there is no accumulation of thoughts, there can be no stronghold.

However, simple discipline is not enough to control the input to our minds. Our minds must be undergoing the renewal process, the path to wholeness, in order for spiritual and mental health to be achieved. As the brokenness in our hearts, the captivities of our spirits, the spiritual blindness, and the wounds are addressed and healed, we are strong enough, and whole enough, to battle the onslaught of thoughts coming our way.

The Sphere of Demons

Lucifer and his angels who rebelled against the Father were thrown down out of heaven into a realm of darkness. This darkness does not refer to lightless regions or areas without physical light:

And the angels who did not keep their positions of
authority but abandoned their own home—these he has
kept in darkness, bound with everlasting chains
for judgment on the great Day.
Jude 6

Rather than this darkness being physical, it is a spiritual darkness, the absence of God's active presence, Who is light:

God is light; in him there is no darkness at all.
1 John 1:5

It is the same spiritual darkness out of which we were rescued.

118

For he has rescued us from the dominion of darkness
and brought us into the kingdom of the Son he loves.
Colossians 1:13

Just as the darkness mentioned in 1 John is not physical but spiritual darkness, so the darkness in Jude is spiritual as well. The sphere of demons is darkness. Therefore, demons have a legal right to reside anywhere there is darkness. The command to walk in the light is the antidote for the encroachment of darkness into our lives:

But if we walk in the light, as he is in the light, we have
fellowship with one another, and the blood of Jesus,
his Son, purifies us from all sin.
1 John 1:7

Seldom does darkness quickly overtake someone. In fact, it comes like dust upon us: slow and nearly undetectable. When I was young, we played baseball every day during the summer. We played all through the day and, after supper, my older brother and I would scurry back out and rejoin the game. We played—completely caught up in the excitement of the game—until we realized we could no longer see enough to hit the ball. The darkness had come so slowly we did not even see it happening. By the time we noticed, it was already dark. Our eyes kept adjusting to the lessened light and we continued to play. So it is with spiritual darkness: it creeps in as we neglect our walk, and relax in our vigilance. Father's warning through Peter is pointed:

Be self-controlled and alert. *Your enemy the devil*
prowls around like a roaring lion looking
for someone to devour.
1 Peter 5:8 (bold mine)

119

Our minds must not only be renewed, but they also must be disciplined to remain alert to prevent the encroachment of darkness in our lives. At some point during that encroachment process, it becomes dark enough for demonic beings to see, and then they move in.

Many denominations teach that it is impossible for believers to be demonized. But according to Jesus' very words, it is possible for believers to yield themselves to spiritual darkness:

See to it, then, that the light within you is not darkness.
Luke 11:35

The light, the presence of God in our lives, is somehow allowed to become darkness. When there is enough darkness (I do not know exactly when enough is enough), we become a place habitable for those relegated to the spiritually dark regions. Well-meaning believers who are convinced darkness and light cannot reside together have challenged me on this point. Yet look at the next verse. It is clear part of our hearts can be light and another part dark:

*Therefore, if your whole body is full of light, **and no part of it dark**, it will be completely lighted, as when the light of a lamp shines on you.*
Luke 11:36 (bold mine)

The battle, then, is the continual process of exposing darkness. It begins at the moment of new birth and continues throughout our lives. The first time we are born, we are born into darkness. When our second birth occurs, we are born into the Kingdom of Light (Colossians 1:12). The process of *"work*[ing] *out* [our] *salvation with fear and trembling"* (Philippians 2:12) is this very thing: exposing and battling the darkness in our hearts, until more and more light is present. Some refer to it as the process of sanctification. We are progressively being set apart from darkness, and being set apart to the light.

> *And that is what some of you were. But you were washed, **you were sanctified**, you were justified in the name of the Lord Jesus Christ and by the Spirit of our God.*
> 1 Corinthians 6:11 (bold mine)

Battling the Darkness

Spiritual warfare begins right here: battling the darkness remaining after salvation and the darkness ever creeping back in to rule our hearts. Here is wisdom: no darkness, no demons. That is where Prophetic Deliverance becomes the weapon of choice for the spiritual warrior intent upon winning not just the battle, but also the whole war.

Chapter 9

General Deliverance Ministry Principles

---•◆•---

We will begin with some general principles for the safety of the participants and the success of deliverance ministry. This list is not intended to be exhaustive, nor is it intended to become sacred. It simply details some of the principles we have developed through trial and error over the years in this ministry.

Never Do Deliverance Alone

Learn and do it as a team. The era when the Lone Ranger approach to ministry was acceptable has passed. The team approach to any sort of ministry is the safest and most profitable method for both the minister and the person being served. If you are married, learn to minister as a couple and work with a team of at least three. This provides a safety net for the team members so just one person's understanding or prophetic word is not held sacred above another's. Father is developing the Body of Christ to be a functioning body, not rogue body parts off doing their own thing.

When doing deliverance, submit the prophetic word and/or vision to one another so it can be tested during the session:

Two or three prophets should speak, and the
others should weigh what is said.
I Corinthians 14:29

If there is only one person there, who will test what you say? Many people who are coming out of former moves of God in the recent past carry with them a pride about their prophetic word and believe their word should be followed without hesitation. Remember this: those who do not submit their prophetic word for testing should not be allowed to speak prophetically to the Church, let alone serve on a prophetic deliverance team.

Never Do Deliverance Without Intercessors

The best way to ensure safety for the team and the client is to recruit people to pray. One way is to be on the intercession team's list in your church, so you are regularly lifted up before the throne. If you do not have an intercessory team in your church, why not start one? There is a great move of God in warfare intercession happening around the world in these times. The way to do it is to first get teaching from one of the many excellent resources available, and then form a team (or teams) to cover your church family and, of course, your deliverance ministry.

Otherwise, ask four or five of your friends to pray for you several days prior, during the session, and for a couple of days after the session. This principle has been learned through many years of being under attack several days before a session, worked over on the day of a session, and annihilated for several days following a session. Intercessors are the warriors of the Body, and they will save your life. If you do not know any, train some from your fellowship and put them to work.

Give the intercessors your schedule, but we recommend you not tell them for whom you are praying. Just tell them when the session begins. This provides for the prophetic nature of intercession to be fully realized. If they know whom you are serving, they may be tied to their natural mind, their natural understanding, praying for only those things they know about the person or about the deliverance team.

The intercessors should be trained to pray over all aspects of the deliverance team. They should cover the person, his or her family, the church family, and the other intercessors. They should be told the time the session begins, but not when it ends. This makes room for the Holy Spirit to lead them beyond the limits of time into the eternal aspect of the warfare. Many times, we have asked the intercessory teams what time they finished praying on a particular evening and their response has been within minutes of the time the session actually closed. Do not limit your teams to the natural way of things. Press them to hear the Spirit and to respond to His instruction.

Never Do Deliverance Without the Full Armor of God in Place

Finally, be strong in the Lord and in his mighty power. Put on the full armor of God so that you can take your stand against the devil's schemes. For our struggle is not against flesh and blood, but against the rulers, against the authorities, against the powers of this dark world and against the spiritual forces of evil in the heavenly realms. Therefore put on the full armor of God, so that when the day of evil comes, you may be able to stand your ground, and after you have done everything, to stand. Stand firm then, with the belt of truth buckled around your waist, with the breastplate of righteousness in place, and with your feet fitted with the readiness that comes from the gospel of peace. In addition to all this, take up the shield of faith, with which you can extinguish all the flaming arrows of the

evil one. Take the helmet of salvation and the sword of
the Spirit, which is the word of God. And pray in the
Spirit on all occasions with all kinds of prayers and
requests. With this in mind, be alert and always
keep on praying for all the saints.
Ephesians 6:10-18

This should be a daily consciousness for every believer. There are a variety of positions regarding the armor, whether it is something coming into place at the moment of salvation and remains, or if we should daily ask for its placement. My understanding is this: as long as it is honoring and glorifying to Jesus, what can it hurt to ask Him about it every day? It is the simple acknowledgment of Jesus as our righteousness, Jesus as the truth, Jesus as our peace, Jesus as our salvation, Jesus as the source and the object of our faith, and Jesus as the Word, the sword of the Spirit. Only when it becomes some sort of lifeless duty or compulsive, superstitious act should it be reevaluated. However, the daily recognition of Jesus as the fullness of our life and the very spiritual armor for the warfare is certainly appropriate.

When performing deliverance, this point is doubly important. When we come in our own strength and power, without acknowledging our Source, we will find ourselves as did the sons of Sceva: *"He* [the demonized man, under the power of the demon] *gave them such a beating that they ran out of the house naked and bleeding"* (Acts 19:16). Praying on the armor is verbal recognition and reminder of our Source, our protection, and our power. The armor is designed specifically for use during spiritual warfare prayer. Notice verse eighteen again:

And pray in the Spirit on all occasions with all kinds
of prayers and requests. With this in mind, be alert and
always keep on praying for all the saints.

125

The armor of God is for intercession. Paul said put on the armor *"and pray."* Although we are proponents of employing the armor for daily living, the point is well made—intercession must be done only with the armor in place.

Never Do Deliverance with an Audience

The more people in the room, the greater chance of problems. When there are too many people in the room, you may find the demons they are carrying become a hindrance to your work with the client. At times, they will try to distract you so something is ignored or overlooked. Other times, they may simply stand against you and multiply the work required to cast out the client's demons. In any case, extra spectators should be avoided.

Any observers should be in the same spiritual position as the team; otherwise, they are at risk, and they put the team at risk. This is especially true when you are first learning. We recommend you have only your team and the client. The only exception would be if you are in a training situation. If you are training a new deliverance team, bring them in a couple at a time and let them observe. Our ministry continually trains and equips new deliverance ministers, so we include extra people in that mode. We include it as part of the apprentice process, but trainees are the only observers we allow.

The foremost reason for a small team is the privacy of the client. Deliverance deals with the deepest, most base portion of people's lives, and we find they are less apt to open up and be vulnerable in front of a sizable group than before just three or four. This is an intensely personal time and should be shared with as few people as possible.

If the person has manifested a spirit in the middle of church service or some other public place, then you must do what you have to do to take care of the situation. The best course of action is to remove the person to a private area and complete the work. Other times, the Holy Spirit may make it clear that you should use it as an instructional opportunity for those who have witnessed the outburst. This should be done as seldom as possible.

On several occasions, we have been put in the position of having to deal with spirits in front of large crowds. On one such occasion, a woman had fallen down in the middle aisle of the church and was convulsing frantically. The pastor directed us into the situation, which, by that time, was completely out of hand. The ruckus had drawn the attention of almost everyone in the church, so it seemed good to us and to the Holy Spirit to show the audience the liberty of deliverance and to wipe away the awe they were experiencing at the power of the unclean spirit. I stepped up to where the lady lay, bent over and tapped gently on her forehead. The lady (Carla) had given over her will to the demon. She had been fighting it for so long she was just tired, so she had given up and let it do what it wanted. As I tapped on her forehead, I kept saying her name. I did not want to talk to the demon; I wanted to talk to Carla. In a few moments, she regained consciousness, and I asked her if she could hear me, and she responded that she could. I asked her if she wanted to be rid of the demon and again Carla responded affirmatively. I asked for her husband (who was trying unsuccessfully to crawl under his seat) to come and sit by her head as her spiritual protector.

Next, I proceeded to instruct the crowd. I asked the right side of the auditorium to begin praying for Carla, for me, and for the other observers. Then, I turned to the other side and instructed them to ask the Holy Spirit to direct them to some portion of Scripture in case I asked for some during the session. Then, I spoke very softly to the unclean spirit, calling it by its functional name, and commanded it to come out.

When it did not move, I asked the Holy Spirit to show me whether there was a generational curse line. Very swiftly, it appeared to me and we used the Sword of the Spirit to sever it. Once that was accomplished, the demon came out without effort and Carla was set free. As the service continued, she lay there for a while and rested. Then she got up and went back to her seat. A few minutes later, she and her very relieved husband came down the aisle for prayer. As she approached, it was clear her countenance was completely different. Even my children who, as pastor's children, had seen nearly every strange event and were never impressed, were astonished at how different she looked.

We had done deliverance in front of a large crowd, but we did it because Carla had already been embarrassed and shamed by the unclean spirit in front of the people. It only made sense to shame the demon in the same manner and to bring glory to God through its public defeat. It returns much of the dignity to the person when the onlookers can witness the transformation. As a general rule, it is good to keep the embarrassment to a minimum by keeping the team small.

Fast and Pray

This should be a lifestyle. Jesus' statement *...this kind goeth not out but by prayer and fasting* (Matthew 17:21 KJV) is a reference to a lifestyle of fasting and prayer, not just single fasting events. As a deliverance team member, you should maintain some pattern of fasting and prayer, so when you meet up with *"this kind"* of unclean spirit, you may cast it out without fanfare.

Within the fasting schedule, you may choose to fast a single meal or completely for the days prior to the session. We recommend you never fast on the day of the session. Fasting makes the body weak, and your weakness can be a place of attack. There have been studies by certain deliverance ministries correlating the work in deliverance with excessive loss of protein from one's system, so it seems prudent to eat and be strong physically the day of the session.

Fasting humbles the body, affording a greater ability to hear God. Because prophetic deliverance is dependent upon hearing God, it is essential fasting be part of the deliverance minister's lifestyle.

Remind the Demons of the Source of Your Authority

Make sure you completely identify the source of your authority. There are many demons who call themselves "Jesus" and many so-called "Christs." We have encountered demons who respond to a command given "in the name of Jesus" with vile humor and stubbornness because they are functioning under that name. Remember, the proper name Jesus is not exclusive to our Lord. During the time Jesus lived on the earth, His name, (*Yeshua*, translated *Joshua* in the Old Testament) was the fifth most common name among Hebrew boys. Throughout history, it has been popular to give male children this name. In fact, one of the most popular names of the past few decades in America is Joshua.

Therefore, it is essential to be as specific as possible when declaring Jesus' name. This is done through a process of narrowing down Whom we are talking about. For example, the name *Bob* is a very popular name in our country. What would happen if we issued a nation-wide ad which read, "Bob, call me." We would certainly be inundated with calls because there are many thousands of Bobs in the country. So the process would have to be narrowed. We could say, "Bob, of the east coast, then, "Bob, of New York," then, "Bob, of upstate New York," then, "Bob, of Chemung County," then, "Bob, of Elmira," then, "Bob, of Maple Street," and then, "Bob, of 319 Maple Street" What we have done is eliminate all the other *Bobs* until there is no question as to which one we are speaking.

The same holds true in deliverance. We use a simple address

in our deliverance sessions so the unclean spirits have no grounds for question. The following is a sample: "We come in the name of Jesus Christ of Nazareth, Son of the Living God, Maker of heaven and earth, Who was put to death, and on the third day rose victorious over death and hell, and after He ascended, is even now sitting at the right hand of the Father, making intercession for us." By the time that kind of address is complete, there is no question there is only One of Whom we are speaking.

Once you have established the source of your authority, it is important you make a clean confession of who you are, and, more importantly, who you are not. Jesus put it very plainly when He said,

Agree with your adversary quickly, while
you are on the way with him.
Matthew 5:25

You are a weak and failing human being. Admit it before the spirits before the spirits speak through your client, accusing you of all the things you have ever done.

There are many stories of this happening, but one has come to me recently from my close friend and coworker, David. He tells of his first encounter with unclean spirits after his conversion in the 1970's. He was asked by a friend to come to his house and pray over an older member of the family who was acting in a peculiar manner. Upon his arrival, David found the woman sitting in front of the television watching Rex Humbard's program. She was sitting there, not enjoying the program, but cursing and blaspheming God. She had been a Christian for some time, so this was a startling sight.

David got her to sit down on the couch and sat opposite her and spoke to what he perceived to be a demon. Sure enough, the demon spoke through the woman, only it came out as a low guttural voice saying, "I know who you are and what you have been doing." Then, the demon spoke through her, telling him all his sins, and it was very accurate. David admits, prior to this encounter, he had been entertaining prideful and judgmental thoughts concerning brothers and sisters in the Lord. He was not living in what might be called 'blatant' sin, but truly, his heart was not in the place it should have been with the Lord. David's response to the demon's outburst was to jump over his chair and run out of the house, shouting over his shoulder, "I'm not in the place I should be to pray for her. You'll have to get someone else."

You see, we come into ministry situations as imperfect human beings, maturing day by day, but nonetheless, imperfect. We have found it is safer to *"agree with* [our] *adversary quickly"* and admit we are weak and failing human beings with no power or authority of our own. If you come as the all-knowing-all-seeing-eye, you will be exposed for the fraud you are. We must walk this out in humility and agree with the true accusations. The greater power is made available when we are working in weakness:

> *But he said to me, "My grace is sufficient for you, for*
> *my power is made perfect in weakness." Therefore I*
> *will boast all the more gladly about my weaknesses,*
> *so that Christ's power may rest on me.*
> 2 Corinthians 12:9

Admit you have no name, no power, no strength, and no dominion of your own. Then, tell the demons Who your source is and Whose power is about to be exerted against them. This will save you all sorts of problems in the session.

Always Speak and Act with Confidence

Demons are like dogs and children: the more you scream,

the more they believe you have no control over them. We watch young mothers trying to handle an unruly child in the grocery store. As the war for control is waged, the mother usually loses her cool and begins to scream threats at the child. At this point, the child instinctively knows he has the upper hand.

The same thing is true for unclean spirits. If you try to cast them out through your fear, they will know and will try to make you give up the fight. If you allow yourself to yell, you will find the demons increasingly defiant and next to impossible to rout. Giving in to fear further debases the client and gives glory to the demon.

Avoid it.

Speak softly and with authority. Remember: demons are not deaf. Through the past century of Pentecostalism and the Charismatic Renewal, a behavior pattern has emerged to identify its participants. It usually includes a lot of noise, shouting, wailing, speaking in tongues, among other things, and, without a doubt, includes casting out demons at the top of one's lungs. It seems a doctrine of yelling has developed.

I will say it again: demons are not deaf.

In fact, they are much like children who know instinctively, if mom or dad is yelling they have lost control. This translates in their minds as fear. If you let them see fear, they will take advantage of it and try to scare you off. The greatest weapon used against us is fear. The ministry of deliverance is not for the faint of heart, especially as you first start out. Our early experiences in deliverance were fraught with great struggles to overcome fear just long enough to get the job done. Before your spiritual authority grows, you will encounter any number of situations when you lose control and the demons manifest, trying to scare the life out of you. One time, we were doing deliverance with a young man we had led to the Lord. We were just learning how to do deliverance, not having read or studied on the subject at all. The demon's functional name was "Unteachable Spirit." We had a team of five plus myself and before we were through, all of us were being thrown around the room as we tried to hold him down. He was growling and barking and we all feared for our lives (or at least a good beating like the sons of Sceva). It wasn't until years later, and many sessions later, we learned we did not have to depend upon our own strength and power to hold anyone down. We learned we had enough authority through Jesus' name we did not have to allow the unclean spirits to manifest at all. Up until that point, we lived in fear and we did deliverance in a fearful manner. Your confidence is not in yourself, it is in the NAME. Never give in to any demonic tactics designed to scare you off.

Use the Gift of Discernment (Distinguishing Between Spirits)

Our procedure for deliverance ministry requires the use of the Gift of Discerning Between Spirits: *"To one there is given through the Spirit... distinguishing between spirits"* (1 Corinthians 12:10).

Discerning Between Spirits is the gift of being able to determine if a spirit is from God or from the dark side. Many misuse it to mean all sorts of discerning. We hear people say, "Oh, he really has the gift of discernment." They are usually speaking about some sort of natural wisdom or knowledge the person has in making decisions or giving advice. Although this is a wonderful thing to be able to do, it is not the Biblical Gift of Discernment, or Distinguishing Between Spirits. This gift is exclusively used in the prophetic realm to see or know a spirit and to determine its origin. We find Jesus using the gift, exclusive of natural wisdom, throughout the Gospels as He cast out demons. Though there might be other uses of the gift, it is the gift of the Holy Spirit used most often for deliverance.

The Gift of Discerning Between Spirits is tied closely to the

Gift of Prophecy, Word of Wisdom, and Word of Knowledge. It is prophetic in nature, meaning the ability to "see" a spirit or to "sense" a spirit is prophetic. It is simply an outgrowth of the dreams or visions mentioned in Joel.

First of all, it is the ability to recognize that a spirit is present. This is done through one or more of a variety of means. Seeing with spiritual eyes is the supernatural ability to actually see spirits and know they are evil, know their names, or know their functions. This ability is not common, but as the last days wear on, I believe we will experience more of this level of the prophetic. Additionally, some may see into the spirit realm with their natural, physical eyes. This is sometimes called an "open vision," that is, having a vision with the eyes open, seeing things as if they were real in the physical realm.

Having a Word of Knowledge is closely tied to this gift, too. It is much like knowing or sensing a demon is harassing an individual, knowing its name, and knowing its function. These two gifts can be blurred together by this kind of definition. Finally, the Word of Wisdom might come into play when one knows not only the demon is present, but how to rid the person of the influence.

In the end, the Gift of Discernment is used exclusively to discern the source of a spirit. 1 John 4:1-6 gives us a deeper understanding of this point:

> *Dear friends, do not believe every spirit, but test the spirits to see whether they are from God, because many false prophets have gone out into the world. This is how you can recognize the Spirit of God: Every spirit that acknowledges that Jesus Christ has come in the flesh is from God, but every spirit that does not acknowledge Jesus is not from God. This is the spirit of the antichrist, which you have heard is coming and even now is already in the world. You, dear children, are from God*

*and have overcome them, because the one who is in you
is greater than the one who is in the world. They are
from the world and therefore speak from the viewpoint
of the world, and the world listens to them. We are
from God, and whoever knows God listens to us; but
whoever is not from God does not listen to us. This is
how we recognize the Spirit of truth and
the spirit of falsehood.*

We use the Gift of Discernment in Prophetic Deliverance because our dependency is upon the Holy Spirit for the answers rather than depending upon either the demon or the client. Many deliverance methods employ asking the demon to identify itself or the client to share his or her problem. The first is treacherous at best, and the second is an act of the natural mind. In fact, we recommend you never get in a conversation with a demon. They have a tendency to draw one in and entice one with hidden wisdom, secrets, or power. Remember, you shouldn't believe anything a demon says; they are liars, because their leader is the father of lies:

*You belong to your father, the devil, and you want
to carry out your father's desire. He was a murderer
from the beginning, not holding to the truth, for there
is no truth in him. When he lies, he speaks his native
language, for he is a liar and the father of lies.*
John 8:44

Prophetic Deliverance cannot be accomplished through any other means than through the Gifts of the Holy Spirit. Practice using all of them, from the Word of Knowledge, to the Word of Wisdom, to prophecy, to tongues and interpretation. But especially develop your use of the Gift of Discerning Between Spirits.

135

Be Gentle

Stop abusing the abused. The level of abuse associated with diagnosing whether there are demons present is staggering. I have personally witnessed well-meaning ministers and altar personnel screaming at people who have responded to an altar call. I have seen people strike others in the name of deliverance. All this posturing is unnecessary and abusive to the person coming for help. When a person is demonized, it is clear he or she has been abused by the demons long enough and doesn't need a minister exacerbating the situation with verbal or physical abuse.

During a meeting one time, a woman responded and came forward for prayer. All at once, the person who had stepped in to pray for her began to yell, "Come out!" over and over again. The poor woman was weeping and shaking as the helper kept yelling at her. I had been playing with the worship team, so the whole thing took place right in front of me. Having no authority to do anything about it, I simply watched as he yelled and she cried. It got pretty loud, so the preacher, who was praying for others at the other end of the altar area, pointed at me and then at the situation. We were operating under his authority in the meeting, so I was then authorized to step in. As I did, the helper actually hit the woman in the stomach very hard while yelling, "You come out!" The woman began to retch, as if she were going to throw up right there on the new carpet. When this happened, the helper yelled, "Yes! Yes! Yes! You're coming out!" and he asked for a bucket to catch the oncoming vomit. At that point, I edged past him and patted the woman on the top of the head. She was now bent over at the waist with violent dry heaves. I said softly, but with authority, "We're not going to have any of that. Stand up!" She immediately stopped retching and stood up. Trying to get her attention, I kept tapping her, now on her chin, and asking her name. As I did so, the helper hollered, "Yes! What is your name? You're not Legion! What's your name?" I said, "No, what's *your* name, ma'am?" Someone told me her name, and I said, "Sarah? Sarah?" until she calmed down enough so we could work to get her eyes open. Once that happened, I asked her if she wanted to get rid of the thing torturing her and she stumbled out a weak, "Yes." I asked her to repeat after me that her body belonged to Jesus, but her tongue would not work. She kept trying, but the unclean spirit kept twisting her tongue so all that came out was mumbling. The Holy Spirit opened my spiritual eyes so I could see the demon sitting on her head. I stepped close to the woman and told her I was about to command the spirit off her head so she could talk. She nodded in agreement and I went to work. Within seconds the demons was gone and she could repeat after me, "Jesus Christ is in control of my body."

As I called our deliverance team in, the woman fell down under the power of the real Holy Spirit. She lay there quietly, so the helper knelt down, slapped her on the stomach and yelled, "Come out!" again. I leaned over and said to him, "They're gone. Now let's do some healing." Our team came in and ministered to her brokenness, and she recovered nicely over the next few weeks.

What is the point? It is very simple and very difficult all at once: Stop abusing the abused! These people have been under the influence of the Evil One and have reaped severe consequences from that influence. Why is it our religious learned behavior drives us to further abuse the person in the name of deliverance? I think our religious pride forces us to know the answer to everything. Yet when faced by the profound unknown of the spiritual realm, we fall back on instinct to handle the situation. The learned behavior we have seen, generally on television, is then our only source of help. So we leap up in the air and shout at the top of our lungs just like our favorite televangelist. That is all we know, so we perpetuate learned behavior in our churches and in our families.

Another answer is just as simple: fear! When dealing with

the unknown, something we know is there but cannot see, something that is higher on the creation scale than we, higher in power and in intelligence, we give in to the same fear we knew as little children in our dark bedroom when we knew the boogie man was in the closet or snakes were under the bed. It's the same fear. Our breath gets short, our eyes bulge, and our mouths go on autopilot. I am convinced most of what little children see in the dark is real. I believe one of the plans of the Enemy is to instill fear of the spirit realm in hearts and minds of children, a fear so deep, they carry it into adulthood so we are primed to reject the drawing of the Holy Spirit toward salvation.

A basic rule for deliverance is this: be quiet. In fact, a firm whisper is powerful. Do not give in to fear; do not follow the learned behavior you have seen modeled. Do not abuse and embarrass the person by yelling at him or the demon, or hitting him. Demons are not human, nor are they hard of hearing. Demons are only moved by true spiritual authority. You, your vocal commands, or your pomposity does not move them. They are attached to the person by legal authority, and only a higher authority will move them away; therefore, it is essential we operate in that higher authority. Jesus retrieved it through the cross and the empty tomb. Do not make it of no effect by overacting your part in the deliverance process.

Chapter 10

Our Deliverance Model

———————◆•◆———————

A s I lay out the model we use for doing deliverance, let me
assure you, we do not believe it is the only way to cast out
demons. However, it is the safest, both for the client and the
team, and the gentlest model we've ever seen. What follows is
the detailed model my wife and I have developed over many
years of deliverance ministry. Those who work with us have
adapted it to fit their own language, style, and personality.
However, we feel strongly the main points should be covered
in some manner for the safety of the workers and client, and for
effectual deliverance to result.

The Setting

The location for a deliverance session may be as varied as
the types of people coming for ministry. We have done sessions
in various parts of church buildings, in houses, in tents, out of
doors, in hotel rooms, and even in the lobby of a hotel. As a
general rule, we try to keep the location and setting as informal
as possible to help the client to be as comfortable as possible.
The best place is probably the living room of someone's house.

However, we try not to do deliverance at the client's house. It's safer in the team's spiritual territory.

No matter the location, we set up the space with the team in a circle around a chair for the client. The spirit realm is at least three-dimensional so it is important to cover all angles around the client. The client's chair will face the team leader's chair. The team leader is the traffic director for the session. He or she will work through the model while the rest of the team listens to the Holy Spirit.

Worship

We begin the session with worship just because we love to worship. Our ears, the client's ears, and the demon's ears all must hear that what we do is about *Father*, and not about us. Worship sets the tone for our time together. Deliverance is an act of worship, of acknowledging Father as our focus; not demons, not the team, and not the client.

We begin by taking time to acknowledge the Great I Am. Of course, worship and praise are two different matters. Worship is being occupied with Who God is, and praise is being occupied with what He has done. We take time to focus upon Him, magnifying Him and exalting His name and reveling in His sovereignty. There have been times when His presence comes in so strongly we have been carried away in worship, but in the normal deliverance session, we briefly enjoy the time with Him and move on.

Establish Protection

Once we have worshiped enough, we enter a very important part of the session. In Psalm 34:7, the Psalmist tells us *"The angel of the Lord encamps around those who fear him, and he delivers them."* Through years of experiencing the repercussions loosed against us after deliverance sessions, we have learned those attacks can be minimized and even eliminated altogether by setting up a perimeter of protection. In the early days of learning to do deliverance, we developed our method by trial and error (mostly by error). When a session was scheduled, the attacks would begin sometimes three days before the session and continue for two or three days following. These attacks came in a variety of forms, from instigated fights between family members, sickness, headaches, appliances breaking down, cars refusing to run, church people in an uproar, and similar unpleasantries. Certainly, these kinds of things happen as part of life, but the intensity and regularity of the destruction was too coincidental to dismiss as normal.

Therefore, we believe it is essential for the safety of all concerned that protection should be established wherever the possibility of revengeful repercussions might occur. For each client, team member, and intercessor we establish protection over the following areas:

- **Families**. We mention children, extended families and church family. People have spiritual and relational connections, so we make sure that connection is not used as a reason for attack.
- **Homes**. We have witnessed houses and property being destroyed by revengeful demons following the deliverance of their owner.
- **Places of business**. They do not have to be spoken by name, only in a general sense.
- **Deliverance location**. We ask angels to encamp around the building and especially the room in which the deliverance is being done. We pray a safe sanctuary be created by angels standing all around the place, above and below included. We want the room to be impenetrable

141

from the outside and inescapable from the inside. This is, of course, relating to the spirit realm. We do not want additional demonic beings entering the premises and causing problems. In like manner, we do not want the demons inside to be able to escape and wait outside for the client. We want to cast them out permanently.

- **Intercessors.** We especially ensure the intercessors are covered. They are the ones doing the real warfare. The attacks upon them are fierce.

- **The client and team members.** We ask the angel of the Lord to protect us as we work and after we leave.

Please do not minimize this step as being overly dramatic or paranoid. We are convinced the Western Church is in the state it is in because we do not take the onslaught from the spirit realm seriously.

From time to time, Father allows some sort of attack to sneak through just to remind us of its importance. Several years ago, I bought a program car (just one year old with low mileage, having been used by a leasing company). One day we were doing deliverance with a couple, and as I prepared to send the demons out of the room, it occurred to me there were people in the next room in the direction I normally sent the demons. I quickly changed direction, pointed out toward the street and commanded, "Get out of our territory in that direction." The next day we went out to get in the car and it would not start. When the mechanic checked it out, he told me what was wrong with it, exclaiming, "It's impossible for that to happen to a car as new as this." Immediately, the Holy Spirit spoke to my heart and said, "You sent that ruler-level unclean spirit right over where your car was parked without establishing protection over it." That little glitch in my thinking cost me four hundred dollars.

Command the Demons

The team leader proceeds by commanding any demon within the sound of his or her voice to remain still and quiet so there are no manifestations. Demons are commanded to stand very still, unmoving, and told not to speak to the client or the team, either in the spirit or through the client's mouth. Paying close attention to what is happening in the natural and in the spirit realm, we have at least one member of the team keep her eyes open at all times to make sure the person does not give in to the demon's power and manifest in any way. Should the person manifest, we merely tell the person to resist the spirit's influence, and then we command the spirit to be quiet.

Next, we inform the demons of the source of our authority. We are very specific. Here is where we narrow down which "Jesus" we are addressing. The following is similar to what I have said in hundreds of sessions:

> "We come in the name of Jesus Christ of Nazareth, Son of the Living God, Maker of heaven and earth, Who was put to death, and on the third day rose victorious over death and hell, and after He ascended, is even now sitting at the right hand of the Father and is making intercession for us."

Before we move forward, we take a moment to admit our weaknesses to the spirits involved, telling them we are weak and failing human beings with no power or authority of our own. Then we remind them we do not come in our own name or authority, but in the name of Jesus Christ of Nazareth, Son of the Living God.

We do not operate under our own authority. We embrace our own weakness and allow Father to use it to reveal His own power:

For when I am weak, then I am strong.
2 Corinthians 12:10b

Finally, we reinforce that no manifestations will be allowed. The demons are commanded not to speak through the client; they are not to move either through the client or in the room; and they are not to harass the client nor the team members.

Ask the Holy Spirit

The Gifts of the Holy Spirit are the tools in our toolbox for doing the work of the ministry. All of the twelve gifts in 1 Corinthians 12 are available for every believer to use, as the Spirit sees fit, and as the need arises. At this point in the session, we ask the Holy Spirit to manifest His gifts as needed. He is the One on Whom we rely because He knows exactly what will be required to set people free.

First, we ask for any of the word gifts—word of knowledge, word of wisdom, prophecy, tongues, or interpretation. It is most important to ask specifically for the Gift of Discerning of (distinguishing between) Spirits.

We then ask the Holy Spirit to reveal the name of the chief or ruling spirit that is present. This information will always come through one of the veins of the prophetic: visions, dreams, spiritual sight, knowing, impressions, Word of Knowledge, or prophetic word.

To say this takes practice is an understatement. That is why our teams undergo intensive training in both deliverance and the prophetic. Still, with some work, team members are ultimately able to cut through their own thoughts and opinions and move straight to the task. It is important to note we are not looking for all kinds of prophetic understanding. We ask the Holy Spirit specifically for the name of the chief and ruling spirit. The next section will help clarify how we come to the place of getting past all the distractions to find the name alone.

Bring the Mind Under Submission

Our own thoughts, opinions, ideas, and experience (or lack thereof) are a hindrance to Prophetic Deliverance. We must come to the place where we can hear the voice of the Spirit of God without fail. Every client's life depends upon it. The first step in this process is to take all of our thoughts into captivity and make them obedient to Jesus. Our intention, once our minds are under submission to the Holy Spirit, is to actually have the mind of Christ active in us:

> *But we have the mind of Christ.*
> 1 Corinthians 2:16

Our clients do not need to hear from us; they need to hear from the Holy Spirit of God. So we take our thoughts into captivity and make them obedient to Jesus Christ:

> *...we take captive every thought to*
> *make it obedient to Christ.*
> 2 Corinthians 10:5b

Each time something is seen the thought must be submitted to Jesus in a simple prayer. The team may see a video or a still picture in his or her mind or hear the Holy Spirit speak the name(s) of the demon(s), or sense the name of the demon. In any case, it must be submitted to Jesus thusly: "I take that thought into captivity and make it obedient to Jesus Christ. If it is from You, Lord, please bring it back. If not, then I let it go forever."

If the thought returns, this process must be repeated at least three times before it may be shared with the team:

> *Every matter must be established by the*
> *testimony of two or three witnesses.*
> 2 Corinthians 13:1

Then, as each team member shares, the name of the chief and ruling spirit is established in the same manner—through the testimony of two or three witnesses.

Discern the Name of the Chief Demon

The team's responsibility is to ask three questions:

1. If there are demons present, what is the name of the chief and ruling spirit?
2. Is there a Generational Curse Line?
3. Is there a religious spirit?

We begin by asking the Holy Spirit for the functional name of the chief and ruling demon. We wait for team members to write down what they are hearing from the Holy Spirit. We write it down so there is complete integrity within the team and written confirmation for the client. Each team will have a scribe whose responsibility it is to take notes of the entire session.

Each team member will share what he or she has written. Once the team leader has found the *"testimony of two or three witnesses"* (Matthew 18:16) within the team and is confident it is accurate, it is time to proceed.

We will not proceed until there is sufficient corroboration from the team. If there is no agreement, we will back up and wait on the Holy Spirit again. This is not an indication of failure. Our being human has a tendency to mess up what might otherwise be a perfect process. Once in a great while, the leader, having not received any other corroboration, must proceed upon the witness he has received. This is dangerous and isn't attempted unless absolutely necessary.

Here we need to address the term "functional name." The name of a demon rarely appears to be a proper name. Rather, we understand them as functional names; that is, demons are identified by their function in harassing the individual. There are times when their proper name is given, but it is usually impossible to pronounce because it is in some strange angelic language. Scripture shows demons can be identified by their function:

Then Jesus asked him, "What is your name?"
*"My name is **Legion**," he replied, "for we are many."*
Mark 5:1-20 (vs. 9 shown) (bold mine)

And it came to pass, as we went to prayer,
*a certain damsel possessed with a **spirit of divination***
met us, which brought her masters
much gain by soothsaying...
Acts 16:16 KJV (bold mine)

*For God did not give us a **spirit of timidity**,*
but a spirit of power, of love and of self-discipline.
1 Timothy 1:7 (bold mine)

For example, it is not so much a "spirit of alcohol" we are encountering as much as a spirit using alcohol to control, harass, and abuse the person. A spirit of fear operates by loosing fear into the life of the person. It is not the demon's proper name. It is like people calling someone "Pastor." He might respond to that name, but his mother didn't take one look at him in the hospital at the time of his birth and say, "Hello, Pastor." His birth certificate says "Larry" because it is his proper name. "Pastor" is a designation of his function, or what he does.

We always make sure we have discerned the name of the chief demon. We do not rely upon the spoken word of the client or the voice of the demon speaking through the client. If we approach the demons through what they say, we may get the name of a demon, but generally, they will give the names of the weakest among them first. Then we must work our way, sometimes through hundreds of demons, to the chief demon. It would be like the police knocking on the door of a room with ten criminals inside. If the police demanded, "Whoever is in there, come out," the crooks would fight among themselves and would throw out the weakest among them to satisfy the demand. If the police were unaware of the others inside, they could arrest the one who came out and be satisfied they had accomplished their task.

So it is with deliverance. If we just command blindly what we know from an interview with each client, or what a demon tells us, most of the time the ruling demon will toss out the weakest of those serving under him. This is why we often get folks coming for deliverance who have undergone deliverance in some other form before. If the chief and ruling demon is not ejected, then, while some deliverance has occurred, the sufferer cannot be fully free.

If team members depend upon empirical evidence in place of discernment, they could go away thrilled they had cast out an unclean spirit, but the worst of the spirits would still be in the person. Therefore, we rely upon what the Holy Spirit is speaking rather than upon any other source.

Generational Curse Line

The second question addresses the spiritual attachment to one's ancestors. All humans have Generational Curse Lines since none of us were born in a vacuum.

*Surely I was sinful at birth, sinful from the
time my mother conceived me.*
Psalm 51:5

Physical attributes are passed down from generation. You may look like your father, or have your mother's weird toes, or you and all your brothers are bald, just like your grandfather. You act just like your uncle Pete or have the same sense of humor as your grandmother. In many ways, the way you behave is determined by those who came before you. When you go to a doctor for the first time they demand a family health history because genetic propensities are passed down through your generations. Weaknesses are passed down as well. Alcoholism and other addictive issues, a violent temper, or other character issues run in some family lines. A Generational Curse Line carries all these aspects with the addition of the spiritual. The spiritual nature of your family tree—whether wicked or righteous—is passed down from generation to generation.

Likewise, if your ancestors lived righteously and pursued Father with vigor, your generational line will show the evidence:

*You shall not bow down to them or worship them; for
I, the Lord your God, am a jealous God, punishing the
children for the sin of the fathers to the third and fourth
generation of those who hate me, but showing love to a
thousand generations of those who love me
and keep my commandments.*
Exodus 20:5-6

We call this the Punishment Crescendo. The generational line runs backward through the generations of sin and provides power to the resident demons. Let's break it down for better understanding. We begin with father #1 (we know there is only one father #1 and he is Adam; but for the sake of this discussion, we will begin at some arbitrary point in the generations of a family). Here's a model of the generations:

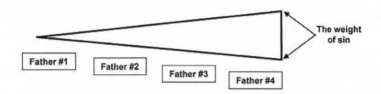

Father #1 carries the weight of his own sin. His son, father #2, carries not only his own sin, but also is weighted down with the sin of his father. The next generation, father #3, enters the world carrying the sin of his grandfather (father #1), the sin of his father (father #2) in addition to his own sin. By the fourth generation of this family, father #4, the weight of sin becomes nearly unbearable. Father #4 must carry the effects of the sin of the three generations before.

All of it together becomes his burden to bear. As bad as that is, what happens when we look one more generation further? Father #4's cumulative sin burden is four generations deep, and he then passes that burden to his son, father #5. Although the Scripture says the sin is passed down through the fourth generation of the family, the weight cumulative total is many generations deep. Is it any wonder America is in the shape it is in? Is it any wonder why civilizations throughout history never last? The total punishment for sin always grows to the breaking point, and then the civilization collapses. Some have lasted for hundreds of years, but ultimately the punishment crescendo breaks the back of the system upon which it rests, and the civilization disintegrates and fades into history.

Let's examine how this issue affects us personally. For example, a person's great grandmother may have been a functioning witch. There are a variety of curses following this person's lineage. As a result, the children and grandchildren usually suffer from an inability to feel the love of God. They may also suffer physical consequences of the grandmother's indulgences. Cancers, diabetes, or other incurable diseases are often associated with this kind of Generational Curse Line. This curse may flow down through the generations, providing psychic abilities or an overwhelming draw into the dark arts. Descendants find themselves dabbling in all sorts of evil, they feel powerless to stop themselves. When deliverance comes and the curse line is severed, the light of God comes to provide the genuine to replace witchcraft, which is simply false spiritual authority. Sometimes the influence is subtler and may affect the client in attitudes or emotions. Although it may be difficult to be precise as to the effect, once the curse line is discovered, it must be broken.

These curses may have been spoken in foolishness, but were more likely passed down intentionally through the rites of one of the secret orders so prevalent throughout history. Secret orders such as Freemasonry actually demand the participant call down curses on themselves and their descendants, dedicating them to one demonic source or another. As a result, the following generations are then plagued with all sorts of illnesses, attitudinal problems, and spiritual darkness. These lines must be severed before the person can be set free from the demonic influences.

Generational curse lines are broken through the use of the Sword of the Spirit, the Word of God (Ephesians 6:17). The Holy Spirit informs the team of the presence of the curse line and its members are adept at quickly finding Scripture as the Holy Spirit speaks it to them. Quoting is fine, but we have found the Holy Spirit will send the members to specific portions not on the list of Scriptures one normally memorizes.

Rather than relying upon canned memorization, it is more powerful to hear what the Holy Spirit has to say directly for that client. The "seeing" team member(s) watch the curse line as the other team members read Scriptures one after another. This repetitive use of the Sword of the Spirit works much like the chopping action of an ax. Through the years, I have watched as the Sword appears in the spirit realm and chops straight through the curse line, saws it, whittles it or in some other fashion cuts the line. We are not bound to only one way. Father is the God of variety. We just make sure the line is broken.

Sometimes, the Holy Spirit will prompt us to have clients repeat a prayer of renunciation. We assure we're not asking them to renounce their family. It is renouncing the curse itself. Once the line is broken, we release the Blood of the Lamb upon the point of attachment to heal the "door." I usually see it like the stump of a tree on the back. As the Blood comes, I see it wash the stump right off so there is no evidence it was ever there.

Religious Spirit

A religious spirit drives the person into performance as opposed to relationship. Ostensibly, religion is about what one does: I will be accepted by Father if I go to church more, read my Bible more, witness more . . . more, more and more *doing*. While these activities are not bad, doing or not doing any of them has no effect upon our acceptance into Father's family. We are accepted by faith alone, faith in Jesus Christ as Savior. The on-going presence of a religious spirit feeds the sense of rejection we feel when not measuring up.

Religious spirits almost always appear around the feet of the client, a metaphor for its function: to hinder the person's spiritual walk. They may appear as vines or chains, or the person may be standing in deep sand or mud; in any case, these are different pictures for the same thing.

The team must address and cast out the religious spirit

separately since the religious nature of the unclean spirit will not submit to any other's authority, even other more powerful demons.

The presence of a religious spirit is determined by the same *"testimony of two or three witnesses"* and is cast out after the Generational Curse Line is broken and the chief and ruling spirit is gone.

Cast the Demon Out

There is always one demon in authority over the person coming for deliverance. The hierarchy of the spirit realm demands it is so. Consequently, we find it unnecessarily wastes time to cast each demon out one after the other until the chief is found. We are asking the Holy Spirit to reveal the name of the chief spirit so we can then command any other spirit under its authority to go with it as it is cast out. It is not necessary to speak every name the team has written down. Most times, team members will hear several names and not be able to distinguish which is the ruler. The team leader must listen for the testimony of two or three witnesses to establish which is the chief.

When the functional name of the ruling spirit has been determined, it is vital the team leader act in authority and command the demon to leave immediately. Through the prophetic, the team will know it has gone. The seer(s) on the team will be able to see when the spirit leaves; the "knower(s)" will be assured he is gone; and the "sensor(s)" will sense it is gone and can give confirmation. The team leaders do not shout or get all worked up; they will simply command it to go.

We always choose a direction to send the demon(s) as they are cast out. It doesn't really matter which way, other than we have found it counterproductive to send the spirit in the direction of the client's house.

Turn on the Light

Up until now, we have been working in spiritual darkness. The client is filled, or partially filled, with darkness and the demon himself is dark. As soon as the Curse Line has been severed and the unclean spirit is cast out, we immediately ask the Holy Spirit to come as light:

> *God is light; in him there is no darkness at all.*
> 1 John 1:5

The seeing member(s) look to see if there is any darkness visible; the knower(s) ask for confirmation from the Holy Spirit; and the sensor(s) get a sense of light or residual darkness. When the Holy Spirit opens up the light, the dark places, if there are any left, will stand out. If we see some darkness, we take time to discern what it is and remove it (cast out more demons, or deal with it when the healing takes place at the end). Each member of the team will confirm there is no darkness left. When there is just light, this is an indication the deliverance session is over.

Chapter 11

The Path to Wholeness

‒‒‒‒‒‒‒◆‒◆‒◆‒‒‒‒‒‒‒

Wounded Spirit and Emotions

In terms of the time commitment, the deliverance session itself is the easy part. It may take all of fifteen or twenty minutes to receive deliverance, but it takes months and even years to recover from the *effects* of the demonization. We have found that life, itself, bruises the spirit of the person. Demonization is the parasite infecting those wounds and draws the very life out of the person. We now return to our foundation to find instruction for ministering healing to the damaged areas of the client.

> *The Spirit of the Lord is upon me, because he hath*
> *anointed me to preach the gospel to the poor; he*
> *hath sent me to heal the brokenhearted, to preach*
> *deliverance to the captives, and recovering of sight to*
> *the blind, **to set at liberty them that are bruised.***
> Luke 4:18 KJV (bold mine)

> *The spirit of a man will sustain his infirmity; but a*
> *wounded spirit who can bear?*
> Proverbs 18:14 KJV

A cheerful heart is good medicine,
but a crushed spirit dries up the bones.
Proverbs 17:22

This is damage—a wounded, crushed spirit—at the core of the person. It is beyond a broken heart, which is emotional in nature. It is beyond mental stress. The very spirit of the person is damaged. It robs one's personality, and masks are created to cover the brokenness.

The presence of the unclean spirits will have damaged the person's emotions as well as his or her spirit. The person will have suffered a broken heart which, left untreated, will invite more and more brokenness. The person's emotions may be out of control or numb. He may be a slave to his emotions as evidenced in a variety of ways such as overreacting in anger, weeping too easily, being very thin-skinned or touchy, or living under an overwhelming sadness. The remedy for this depth of brokenness cannot be found in easy fixes or even through counseling. It is only found in the supernatural healing power of our Heavenly Father.

Prayer for the Wounded Spirit

In the story of the Good Samaritan, the Samaritan saw a man lying beaten by the road and did some ancient first aid. He poured wine and oil into his wounds. The wine acts as an antiseptic, which cleanses the wounds. The oil acts as a healing agent. Then the Samaritan wrapped the man's wounds, took him to an inn and left him in the care of an inn keeper:

He went to him and bandaged his wounds, pouring on
oil and wine. Then he put the man on his own donkey,
took him to an inn and took care of him.
Luke 10:30-37 (Vs. 34)

156

Wine is a symbol of the blood of Jesus shed on the cross, cleansing us from sin. Oil is a symbol of the Holy Spirit, our agent of healing. These two are released upon a person's soulish areas and upon his or her spirit. This is not to be confused with the new creation coming spiritually alive upon receiving Christ as Savior.

The team first releases the wine, the blood of Jesus for cleansing. This is first, just like a wound is to be cleansed before putting on any healing ointment. We call for the blood to come, and as we pray, we are careful to release the virtue from Father. We release the blood for cleansing on three areas, starting with the head. We lay hands on the head as we pray. The head is about the faulty and wounded thinking, beliefs and memories.

Then we pray for the heart. In the Hebrew culture the heart represents the essence of a person's being, the very core. We ask the person to place his or her hand on their own heart and a team member of the same gender places just a couple of fingers on top of his or her hand to be careful to be inoffensive.

Then we ask the person to move his or her hand to the belly. This represents the deepest part of a person's being; the person's crushed and wounded spirit, a place of deep wounds and bruising:

> *The words of a gossip are like choice morsels;*
> *they go down to a man's inmost parts.*
> Proverbs 26:22

> *The spirit of man is the candle of the Lord, searching*
> *all the inward parts of the belly.*
> Proverbs 20:27 KJV

Then we go back to the head and release the oil of the Holy Spirit to heal, again, being very aware of being a conduit of the virtue of Jesus as the Spirit of Jesus flows and brings healing and life to the person in these areas. Oil is then released for healing upon their ears, eyes and mouth to restore the spiritual function these represent: seeing in the spirit realm, hearing in the spirit realm and speaking the matters of the Kingdom. Then we move to the heart again, placing a hand on top of the person's hand and releasing the oil for healing into the wounds of the broken heart and emotions. And then finally we have the person move his or her hand to their belly to loose the healing oil of the Holy Spirit on the inner man.

As we pray for both the cleansing and the healing to be released, we are sensitive to pay attention in the spirit realm to either watch or sense what is going on and only move on to each place as we feel led by the Holy Spirit. We often see or sense the condition of the mind, or the heart, or the inner man, and may see pictures or get information. We often see or sense the presence of the blood of Jesus and the oil of the Holy Spirit as they are applied to each part of the person.

Just as the Samaritan wrapped the man's wounds, we call for the presence of Father to wrap the person like a protective bandage to give protection and safety in a season of healing. Then we leave him or her in Father's care to work His healing in the wounded soul.

As we pray this prayer over people after deliverance we are declaring, "Let the healing begin!" There is much work still needing to happen in the process of healing the wounded soul. We also pray this prayer at the end of each Wholeness Coaching phone call. It is like reapplying a fresh bandage after we are working on the wounds. This prayer can be used with anyone who asks for prayer because people are just wounded. I even pray this prayer over myself when something wounds me.

Here is an example of the Wounded Spirit Prayer:

Father, I thank you for your healing presence. I loose the blood of Jesus for cleansing in the mind, the thinking, and the memories. Bring your cleansing presence in what he (rather than he/she I will just go with he) thinks, believes, and stores in the memories. Let the blood of Jesus flow upon the ears, eyes and mouth, these gates where destruction has entered in through what he has heard, seen and spoken. I loose the cleansing blood upon his heart and his emotions, representing the core of his being. Also, I declare the blood cleansing the deep wounds of his inner man, deep into the hidden wounds and secret wounds, and the old wounds.

Now let the oil of the Holy Spirit come. Bring your healing presence upon the mind, thinking, beliefs and memories. Heal the faulty thinking and lies. Heal the pain stored in the memories. Release the oil of healing into the heart and emotions, the broken places. Bring your healing presence into the deep places of the inner man, into the old wounds, the hidden wounds and secret wounds.

Wrap him in your presence like a protective bandage, watching over him and guarding him in this season of healing. Speak your Word of truth and affirmation into his soul, renewing his mind. I release him into your care because you are faithful to heal, restore and renew. And I declare your Kingdom come and Your will be done in Jesus' name.

This prayer is not just for use after a deliverance session. In fact, it is incredibly healing to pray it over anyone who is in the healing process. We have used it in counseling or when simply coming alongside someone in distress.

Bandage the Wounds

As the wine and oil are completed, this is where we pray the Holy Spirit seals the work done (the act of *"bandaging"*). We loose the anointing, the manifest presence of God upon the healing person.

The final thing we do is ask clients to hold out their hands like they were about to receive a gift, because, guess what? They are! We ask clients to invite the Holy Spirit in afresh, to fill all those areas so recently vacated by the demons. We are not expecting them to speak in tongues or to do anything at all. It is just a moment of safety in the aftermath of deliverance:

When an evil spirit comes out of a man, it goes through arid places seeking rest and does not find it. Then it says, "I will return to the house I left." When it arrives, it finds the house unoccupied, swept clean and put in order. Then it goes and takes with it seven other spirits more wicked than itself, and they go in and live there. And the final condition of that man is worse than the first.
Matthew 12:43-45

Newly freed clients are often concerned about the danger of re-infestation. We often receive a call from them when the learned behavior crops up once again. "I think the demons are back!" they declare. Our answer is always along the lines of, "If they were back, you wouldn't be making this call because they would have convinced you they *weren't* there." The demons cannot return unless they let them return through neglect or outright rebellion. People must choose to be re-infested by the demons. This rarely happens. Father gives them much grace during the recovery period. Do not allow the fear of re-infestation to rob what might otherwise be a great victory.

As for the return of the demons, they will come back to see who is living in you. Remember: you will be inhabited by someone, whether light or dark. So when the demons come back to investigate the living conditions in your being, we want the Holy Spirit to answer the door in His robe and slippers, indicating it is HIS home now.

I learned this lesson in the most negative manner possible. Some people in the church I was pastoring came and asked me to do deliverance with one of their family members. He was a Presbyterian pastor in the local area and was moving to a city a significant distance away to take a new pastorate. During his tenure in our area, he had also worked as a professional counselor for a large Christian counseling center. He was moving not only to take the new pastorate, but also to get away from this commitment.

Initially, I refused to consider deliverance for him (let's call him Al). But after several talks with the family, they convinced me of his commitment to do whatever it took to find freedom.

During our first meeting, I expressed my reservations to Al. I told him I would not do deliverance with anyone who could not commit to attending my church for a minimum of six months for aftercare. It was obvious he was unable to comply with my request. Instead, Al promised firmly, because he had family in our area, he would stay in close contact with me, even making trips to see me for follow up.

The other hurdle I placed in front of him was theological. I warned him that anyone who refused to embrace the fullness of the Holy Spirit (the Baptism, the second work of grace, the indwelling, or whatever your particular group may call it) would be vulnerable to severe attack once the demons were gone. I shared the verse above from Matthew 12, and Al became a convert to my theology on the spot.

My hurdles having been satisfied, I begrudgingly agreed to take him and his wife through deliverance. As we began, I saw the entire physical outline of his body packed full of demons. They looked like those big, black barn flies one might find swarming together in a cow barn. It was so real I told Al to open his mouth to let them out. As he did, I commanded they come out, and out they came, right at me! There were thousands of them, and they were flying into my face. I could feel them hitting my face, neck and shoulders, thousands of them. They flew up my nose and into my ears. I could physically feel them hitting me (my face itches even now as I write this) and I panicked. Just when I was sure I could take no more, they were gone.

In our investigation, we found the demons had entered him through his gift of pastoring and the empathy he felt for each of his counselees over the years. He would literally open himself up to receive familiar spirits from each of the hundreds of patients he had counseled. When we ministered to his wife, we found her in nearly the same state. We cast out several thousand demons that day, and both Al and his wife appeared to be completely clean.

However, after moving to their new pastorate, Al chose to neglect the aftercare to which he committed. He never called me, never wrote or contacted me in any way, and he specifically denied the indwelling of the Holy Spirit.

Within a few months, we received news from Al's family that he had stolen money from his new church. A few weeks later, Al was arrested for running through a downtown park in the nude. Shortly thereafter, he was arrested again when a policeman found him sleeping naked in his car, not a stitch of clothing in sight. Finally, within the next year or so, he was removed from pastoral ministry, divorced from his wife and living with another woman.

When I say we take this portion very seriously, I think it is obvious why. As a result of Al's turning back to his theological roots and neglecting to keep the Holy Spirit of God inhabiting his spirit, he was subjected to seven spirits for each of the thousands who were cast out, each more wicked than the first ones. His brokenness was multiplied, and the demonic influence mounted until neither his mind, his emotions, nor his spirit could handle it. He was crushed under the strain.

Although this is a very dramatic testimony, the re-inhabitation of just one more demon than was there before is nothing at which to sneer. We ensure this theological point is included in our pre-deliverance instructions. We make sure our clients understand the importance of the wholeness process following the session. If they do not agree to the best of their ability, we do not do deliverance for them. Their state is bad now, for sure, but to multiply it by seven times is doing them no favor.

The wounds are bandaged in the presence of the Father and are now ready for healing. Healing in these areas is very much like healing after surgery. There are important steps that must be taken relating to coaching, digging through the source of the hurts, and exposing them to the Light. This takes place through active participation in a variety of nurturing environments such as house groups, support groups, and Katie's Wholeness Coaching. We never let the person simply heal on his or her own.

Post-Deliverance Counseling and Follow-Up

Directly after deliverance, we teach people that this is just the beginning; it is not an end in itself. Deliverance takes only fifteen or twenty minutes; aftercare takes months, even years. Just because the demons are gone does not mean the client will now have a perfect existence. It was the wounded state enabling the person to be demonized in the first place. Rather, he must learn how to live differently since the demons are gone. The person, under the influence of the demon, will have been trained to act and react in certain ways. He will have developed paradigms that must be changed. The Kingdom of Darkness thinking must be routed out and exposed to the Light. He may not know how to act for a while. He may overreact emotionally now that he actually has emotions, although he may not know how to properly use them. He may feel out of control.

Although the demonic influence is gone, the learned behavior will remain. Clients must learn to live without the demonic influence. It must be emphasized—this part may take some

163

time—he must not expect perfection from himself, nor must he be held to some kind of spiritual perfectionism by his pastor or peers. We must learn to live in the grace of God. This seems like simple instruction, but we find it is a key to wholeness after deliverance. The process is simply the exchange of His thoughts for ours.

Our follow-up plan involves coaching calls with clients for several weeks to assist them in walking out this new leg of their journey to wholeness. Where this is not possible, we recommend active transparency with their small group or with whatever inner healing program their church has to offer.

Occasionally, clients do not expose everything needed to get to the chief and ruling spirit. The reason this happens is often a high level of woundedness so pervasive they cannot manage to open it up to the light. When this happens, we will be contacted sometime after the first session for additional help. We will accommodate clients for the second one and maybe a third in the future if they are making measurable progress, but if someone asks for more than that, it is an indication he just wants the attention, or he is not committed to the recovery process. So, for his own safety we will decline additional sessions.

If the client returns for an additional session, it is often seen as a 'peeling of the onion.' We will have cast out the highest ranking demon at whatever level we were allowed to see in the first session and now we move deeper, peeling additional layers of the 'onion' until the actual chief and ruling demons is exposed. The person may simply have now moved forward enough in the wholeness process to trust Father with exposure at a deeper level. Although we can see into the spirit realm, the person must give us permission to expose them to the Light. If he chooses, maybe out of fear or suspicion, to hide his true demonization, we are powerless to find the demons. Most of the time, it is a case of being too wounded or too fearful to let the Holy Spirit search their innermost being. These additional sessions should

164

be attempted only after counseling.

If another session is required, we do it with a warning: the problem may just be a character issue rather than more demons. People frequently want to blame their problems on someone else. The popular phrase of the seventies still rings in my ears as people consistently tell me in so many words, "The devil made me do it." If the person asks for another session, we discuss it with his counselor and pray it through. If we do not feel it is demonic, we help him see it is learned behavior. Learned behavior is exactly what it says: it is the behavior, the way of thinking and doing, which we have learned under the influence of the demon(s).

The Gift of Forgetfulness

Now, before you race to find this gift in the Scriptures, be assured I made it up. In spite of that fact, deliverance ministers should ask Father for this very necessary gift. It is based upon what Father does with our sins:

> *As far as the east is from the west, so far has he removed our transgressions from us.*
> Psalm 103:12

We believe in the phrase: deliver and forget. He has done it for you, do it for your clients and for yourself. There is no possible way to carry all you will know through Prophetic Deliverance and ministering to their wounds. It is too much for any person to carry. This is more than a recommendation: throw it away.

The more sessions we did, the more our minds would clog up with dirty information about the people we had served in deliverance. If we are the storehouse of all the dirt in people's lives, we will soon crumble under its weight. I got to the point where I could not look people in the face because what would come to mind was what they had done, or what had been done to them.

Their destruction was becoming my undoing.

One day, the Holy Spirit spoke clearly to my heart and said, in effect, "Ask me for forgetfulness." I thought about for a bit and the concept became clear. I was not able, in my own strength, to forget what I knew. It was always there to remind me, so the only solution was to ask for it to be removed as supernaturally as it had come. I quickly asked Him for the Gift of Perfect Forgetfulness, and I was amazed at its effectiveness. In the years since that time, my wife is convinced it works too perfectly, affecting the other portions of my life, but we are sure it's well worth it.

People are forever coming up to me and asking me about their deliverance sessions. I am sure some of them are offended when I say I am unable to recall anything about it. But when I gently explain what I have explained in these paragraphs, most of them, although they probably do not really believe me, let me off the hook.

Pay Attention

The final important thing that must be done is…

> ***Be self-controlled and alert.*** *Your enemy the devil prowls around like a roaring lion looking for someone to devour. Resist him, standing firm in the faith, because you know that your brothers throughout the world are undergoing the same kind of sufferings. And the God of all grace, who called you to his eternal glory in Christ, after you have suffered a little while, will himself restore you and make you strong, firm and steadfast. To him be the power for ever and ever. Amen.*
> 1 Peter 5:8-11 (bold mine)

No one should enter deliverance ministry (or any other ministry for that matter) in a slipshod, lackadaisical fashion. It could get you killed. We use the term Spiritual Warfare for a very real and practical reason: people are dying. They are dying and slipping into eternal darkness. Unless we bring them the Light, they have no hope. Move out into the ministry of Prophetic Deliverance confident Father has given all authority and power to His Son and has placed all His enemies under His feet. We only have to believe it is true and take that life-giving Message to the world.

I pray also that the eyes of your heart may be enlightened in order that you may know the hope to which he has called you, the riches of his glorious inheritance in the saints, and his incomparably great power for us who believe. That power is like the working of his mighty strength, which he exerted in Christ when he raised him from the dead and seated him at his right hand in the heavenly realms, far above all rule and authority, power and dominion, and every title that can be given, not only in the present age but also in the one to come. And God placed all things under his feet and appointed him to be head over everything for the church, which is his body, the fullness of him who fills everything in every way.
Ephesians 1:19-23

About the Author

———————————◆·•◆·•◆———————————

Tim Mather, Th.D., is the founder and executive director of Bear Creek Ranch, a retreat center focusing on deliverance and wholeness ministry. He is the author of Out of Bondage: Identifying and Breaking Control Spirits in the Church and Escaping Church: A Guide to Life Outside the Institution. He can be contacted at www.BCRcamp.com.

WHAT'S NEXT?

Read *The Five Wholeness Steps* by Katie Mather for a practical step-by-step process of inner healing.

Is it possible to heal the wounds of the soul before deliverance? One can pursue God and His healing before deliverance, but can only reach as far as the internal saboteur will allow. After deliverance, it is truly possible to expose the broken places and allow God's healing deep in the wounded soul.

The Five Wholeness Steps is a practical guide for dialog between you and God, to bring His healing into the wounded soul after deliverance.

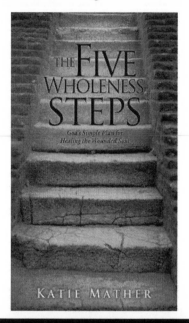

Resources

Books:

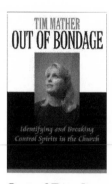

Out of Bondage
by Tim Mather

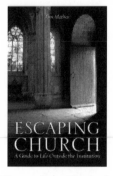

Escaping Church
by Tim Mather

The Five Wholeness Steps
by Katie Mather

Supernatural Superheroes
by Heather Trim

Visit the Bear Creek Bookstore for more information.
www.BCRcamp.com

More Resources

Audio Teachings:

**Upside Down
Kingdom Weapons**
with Tim Mather

Wholeness JumpStart
with Katie Mather